"*Welcome to the Story* reads, we ⸺ ⸺ esting and important character⸺ ⸺ ⸺ ⸺ ⸺ ⸺ ⸺ mystery, striking beauty and hideous ugliness, noble and courageous heroes along with wicked and contemptible villains, all depicting the richness and sweeping breadth of this story. Along the way, one encounters many testimonials from others who likewise have been involved in this story, and the reader is invited to consider how he or she also should enter this story. In the end, Nichols shows how this Story is the story of all stories, since its central character is none other than the King who is over all kings, the Creator and Author of the story in which he plays the leading part. I encourage you to read this story, enter the story, and join in making this Story—the story above all stories—your story."

Bruce A. Ware, Professor of Christian Theology,
The Southern Baptist Theological Seminary

"Nichols has written a delightful and inviting book on how to understand and live out the Bible. The storyline of the Scriptures is sketched in, and the book is full of wise advice on how to read and live out what God requires. I recommend the book with enthusiasm."

Thomas R. Schreiner, James Buchanan Harrison
Professor of New Testament Interpretation,
The Southern Baptist Theological Seminary

WELCOME TO
THE STORY

WELCOME TO
THE STORY

READING, LOVING, AND LIVING
GOD'S WORD

STEPHEN J. NICHOLS

WHEATON, ILLINOIS

Trade paperback ISBN:	978-1-4335-2230-7
PDF ISBN:	978-1-4335-2231-4
Mobipocket ISBN:	978-1-4335-2232-1
ePub ISBN:	978-1-4335-2242-0

Library of Congress Cataloging-in-Publication Data
Nichols, Stephen J., 1970–
　Welcome to the story : reading, loving, and living God's word /
Stephen J. Nichols.
　　　p. cm.
　Includes bibliographical references and index.
　ISBN 978-1-4335-2230-7 (trade pbk.)—
　ISBN 978-1-4335-2231-4 (pdf)—
　ISBN 978-1-4335-2232-1 (mobipocket)—
　ISBN 978-1-4335-2242-0 (epub)
　1. Bible—Reading. I. Title.

　BS617.N45 2011

　220.6'1—dc22　　　　　　　　　　　　　　　　2010045598

Crossway is a publishing ministry of Good News Publishers.

VP		19	18	17	16	15	14	13	12	11
	15	14	13	12	11	10	9	8	7	6	5	4	3	2	1

To the Memory of

Ella Jean Detwiler

My fourth grade Sunday school teacher who
read the story with grace,
loved the story her entire life,
and
lived the story before me and many others.

CONTENTS

Acknowledgments 11

You're Invited 15

1 The Story 19

2 It Was Good: Creation 29

3 Trouble in Paradise: Fall 43

4 Unto Us, a Child: Redemption 55

5 Hope's Comin' round the Bend: Restoration 69

6 The Story within a Story: Peter, Paul, and Mary 91

7 God's Story, God's Glory: Adventures in *Not* Missing the Point 105

8 Loving the Story: What the Bible Does *to* Us 119

9 Living the Story: What the Bible Does *through* Us 131

10 Digging Deeper: This All Sounds Good, but Now What? 147

Cheat Sheet for Reading the Bible 165

Notes 171

General Index 173

Scripture Index 175

Acknowledgments

I WOULD LIKE TO THANK the team at Lancaster Bible College who tackled the freshman course that spawned the idea of writing this book: Penny Clawson, Gordon Gregory, Deb Hinkel, Rick Rhoads, and Dan Spanjer. Thanks for the camaraderie, for the conversations, and for those summertime workshops.

Thanks to those who read parts or all of this, especially Keith and Bev Haselhorst. Who knew that in-laws could be gracious critics? Ned Bustard, Jeff Trimbath, and Gordon Gregory also gave kind encouragement and helpful comments.

Thanks to all my friends at Crossway, who treat their authors like family and make writing a pleasure.

And thanks to my real family, Heidi, Ben, Ian, and Grace. Your graciousness and love know no bounds.

Oh that I knew how all thy lights combine,
	And the configurations of their glory!
	Seeing not only how each verse doth shine,
But all the constellations of the story.

George Herbert, "The H. Scriptures 2"

YOU'RE INVITED

I'VE HAD ONE SMALL brush with the movie business. Well, actually, it really wasn't much of anything, but I enjoy telling the story. My friend Pete Bargas, at The Master's College in Santa Clarita, California, arranged for me to have a tour of the Disney Studios in Burbank, led by our very gracious host Rick Dempsey, vice president for creative at the home of Mickey.

We went into the studio while they were recording the voices for the new Winnie the Pooh movie, visited the animation archives, walked through some of the sets and through stages in warehouse-like buildings as large as football fields, and saw the engineers at work on the sound mixing for one of the shows on ABC.

These were all closed-door places. No tours go where we went. Menacing signs—yes, they exist even at Disney—let us know that we were going where few people get to go, seeing what few people get to see, experiencing what few people get to experience.

I called my wife and kids, and then my mom, letting her know what great honor had befallen her son. I e-mailed my film-studies friend, just to make him feel jealous. It was all very exciting.

To be invited to the Disney Studios, to have your name on a list at the guardhouse gate, to get a special tour by a studio exec, to go behind the scenes to see how these shows that mesmerize us are made, to see firsthand stars and talented people at work, was all something indeed. And that's my small brush with the movie business.

There's something to getting an invitation, especially an invitation to someplace significant or to some special event. A few weeks ago I had a conversation with a veteran Sunday school teacher. Each week she lovingly shapes and molds four-year-olds. She's been at it so long she now receives wedding invitations from her former students. And those invitations are both a delight—despite the fact that those invitations speak of how the sands of time march on—and an honor. Whether it's an invitation to the Disney Studios, to some grand place, or to the wedding of a now grown-up former four-year-old Sunday school student, any possible invitation anyone could receive pales in comparison to the invitation given to us all: *to take and read the very Word of God.*

At one particularly low point in his ministry, Christ shared an intimate moment with his disciples. The day had started off pretty well. There was a crowd of over five thousand who had come to hear him preach. But as the day wore on and Christ offered up some hard teachings, after he performed the miracle of multiplying the loaves and the fish, the crowds walked away in droves. None but Christ and the twelve were left.

Christ turned to the twelve, asking them, "Do you want to go away as well?" Peter, bold and brash as his M.O. had it, spoke up first. He asked, "Lord, to whom shall we go?" Then he answered his own question, "You have the words of eternal life."

When we first meet John Bunyan's wonderful character, Christian, in his classic allegory, *Pilgrim's Progress*, Christian has a book in his hand and a burden on his back. The burden is his sin, and the book is the remedy, the very Word of God, the Bible. Christian's family and friends implore him not to go off on his journey in search of the Celestial City. They vainly reach to pull him back, while he puts his fingers in his ears and sets off running for the gate. "Life, life, eternal life," Christian shouts as he runs.

We have been given a book that is unlike any other book in human history, a book that transcends all human wisdom, all human insight, and all human expertise. We have been given the Word of God, the words of eternal life. And we, all of us, are invited to take up and read these words.

There is no substitute for reading the Bible. But some of us may need a little help to read it better. There are lots of books on reading and understanding the Bible, books that offer methods and skills and techniques. This book does some of that.

There are also lots of theological books that take a step back from individual biblical passages and biblical texts to try to grasp the big picture of what's happening. This book does a lot of that. And there are books that try to stir our hearts and souls to long for and desire to read the Word of God. This book does that, too.

This book invites you to enter in, to participate in, the story of the Bible. To do so, we must first see and grasp the story. We can put a puzzle together much more easily if we are looking at the picture on the box. This book aims to show you the big picture so you can make sense of all the pieces.

One of the books that influenced me early on in my studies was called *He Gave Us Stories*, by Richard Pratt. In the book he points out how God communicated to us originally and primarily in stories. We need to know that God, the transcendent Creator of the universe, sees us and cares for us. So he gave us the story of Hagar in Genesis 16. We need to know that God provides for us even when we are hanging on by the slimmest of threads. So he gave us the story of Abraham, Isaac, and a ram caught in a thicket in Genesis 22. And on it goes.

Pratt was quite right. God gave us stories. As we approach reading Scripture we will use this central theme of story, for the Bible

17

is both a collection of stories and also one grand story, the grand story of redemption. That's the picture on the box. That's what we need to grasp so we can better read God's Word to us.

This isn't simply a cognitive exercise, however. There's more to reading Scripture than merely understanding it. We must also love and, in the words of the psalmist, delight in Scripture. So we'll talk about that, too.

And let's not forget the wisdom of the book of James. Reading Scripture is as much about doing as it is about knowing and loving. So we'll also look at living out Scripture, at entering into the story in such a real and palpable way that we participate in Scripture, that we live Scripture, that we reflect the story of Scripture in our own lives. Scripture is not some treasure to be hoarded. It is to be shared. So we'll also discuss how we might proclaim Scripture. We'll find that we live out Scripture as we serve and proclaim.

Finally, we'll offer some practical tips for reading the Bible. To help out even more, we'll end with a cheat sheet for Bible reading. This is how we enter into and participate in the biblical story—by reading it, loving it, living it, and proclaiming it. For in this story we will find the words of eternal life.

You are invited to take up and read.

1

THE STORY

We are torn out of our own existence and set down
in the midst of the holy history of God on earth.
—Dietrich Bonhoeffer, *Life Together*, 1938

And we thank God constantly for this, that when you
received the word of God, which you heard from us, you
accepted it not as the word of men but as what it really is,
the word of God, which is at work in you believers.
—1 Thessalonians 2:13

GLEN KEANE MAY NOT BE that well known to you,
but his work likely is. He's one of the many animators at Disney
(keeping with my movie business story for a bit longer). He brings
all sorts of animals, characters, and even objects—who could ever
forget the broomsticks in *Sorcerer's Apprentice*?—to life. Among his
many credits stands his animation for *Beauty and the Beast*. Through

Glen Keane's creative mind and skilled hands, he hurriedly sketched out the frames of the transformation of the beast into the prince.

And as he sketched away at his art desk, he was guided by a verse from Scripture. The verse Keane had written out and that he had taped across the top of his desk was 2 Corinthians 5:17, "Therefore, if anyone is in Christ, he is a new creation. The old has passed away; behold, the new has come." At an in-house meeting at Disney just before the release of the movie, Glen Keane shared about what inspired him as he worked and as he crafted the images that would depict the scene where he turned the beast into the prince. It was, he said, nothing more than his attempt to depict the transformation brought about by Christ, the transformation that takes a sinful human being, a beast, and transforms him into a prince—a transformation in which the old passes away and the new, the all-new, comes.

This story of transformation, of redemption, is the greatest story ever. Versions of this story of redemption pop up all over culture. You'll find them in movies like *Beauty and the Beast*, in books, and in songs. Who doesn't want to see the fallen hero restored? Who doesn't hold out for redemption? Who doesn't want to see the beast transformed? The Bible gives us the ultimate story of transformation. It is not just the story of my transformation or yours. The Bible tells the story of *our* transformation.

THE BIBLE AS *THE* STORY, THE BIBLE AS *OUR* STORY

In 1935, the German National Church threw its support behind the Nazi party. Troubling to many in the church, a group met at the city of Barmen, drawing up The Barmen Declaration and forming what came to be called the Confessing Church. This new church would confess allegiance to Christ only, not to the state. The Confessing Church also decided to establish four seminaries to train pastors for this new movement.

They settled on the city of Finkenwalde, then in Germany and now in Poland, as the place for one of these seminaries. And they settled on Dietrich Bonhoeffer as its director. He was just about to turn thirty and already had an impressive career. The seminary existed for just over a year before the gestapo shut it down, arrested most of its students, and sent others into hiding. Bonhoeffer went to his parents' home and wrote a book about it all, *Life Together*. In a few years, Bonhoeffer himself would be arrested, and in a few years still he would be hanged at Flossenbürg concentration camp, just a handful of days before that camp would be liberated. All of this is to say that what Bonhoeffer has to tell us in *Life Together* is well worth hearing.

Bonhoeffer stresses many ideas in the book, with that of *community* topping the list. "Christianity means community," he tells us. For Bonhoeffer, community circles around our *common union* that we have in Christ. Living together, learning together, worshiping together, suffering together, Bonhoeffer and his students learned a great deal about true community.

One thing Bonhoeffer learned, though, is that community is not isolated to one time and one place. The Christian community is global, blowing apart any geographical boundaries. But, Bonhoeffer also learned that the Christian community is historical, transcending the barriers of time. In fact, the Christian community stretches all the way back to the pages of the Bible itself. The biblical story is *our* story. It is not the story of biblical characters written down for us. It is the story of us, because we are all part of the Christian community.

Bonhoeffer commends this idea of community as the fundamental way we read and engage God's Word. While it is an ancient word to an ancient people of different languages and customs and times and places, it is also at the same time God's word directly to us. It is the Word that, as Paul puts it, is at work in us, not just the Word at work in believers scattered about the ancient city of Thessalonica (1 Thess. 2:13; see also 1 Pet. 1:22–25).

Here's how Bonhoeffer expresses the way in which the Word of God becomes our story:

> We become a part of what once took place for our salvation. Forgetting and losing ourselves, we, too, pass through the Red Sea, through the desert, across the Jordan into the promised land. With Israel we fall into doubt and unbelief and through punishment and repentance experience again God's help and faithfulness. All this is not mere reverie but holy, godly reality. We are torn out of our own existence and set down in the midst of the holy history of God on earth. There God dealt with us, and there He still deals with us, our needs and our sins, in judgment and grace.

Then he adds a final exclamation point, "Only in the Holy Scriptures do we learn to know our own history."[1] The Bible is our story because we are part of and connected to the Christian community. So far we have been putting the emphasis on *our*. We also need to emphasize *story*.

THE STORY OF THE BIBLE

I'm a morning person and I love to teach classes starting at 7:30 a.m., a challenging hour for college students. I can tell when I'm going to lose them, and I have found that's always a good place for a story. Any story will work. The drooping eyelids lift and they slowly return to the land of the living. I understand enough about my students to know that they love stories. In fact, we all love a good story.

God has full wisdom and perfect understanding of us. He knows exactly what we need. So he gave us stories. The Bible is one grand story by, from, and, ultimately, about God. What we have stumbled upon here in the Bible is the greatest story of all time. It's the story of redemption, the story of God calling out and making a people for himself. It is also a true story, the truest of them all. What can be better than that?

Well, there is one thing. The story of the Bible is not only the greatest story and not only the truest story. It is also the only story that makes sense of our lives. To put it another way, the Bible has *existential significance*. The Bible gives meaning to all our lives and to every inch of our lives. It alone makes sense of what happens to us. The Bible alone makes sense of all the confounding and confusing things we experience.

Stories played a crucial role in ancient cultures. As people gathered around the fire, the older generation would tell stories to the younger. They would tell these stories to entertain—even ancient people had challenges in putting the kids to bed. They would tell these stories to instruct, to explain how various people were to act in the culture, to explain the roles they were to play. And in the telling of these stories they would know of their place in the tribe and their place in the universe. The oral traditions and folklore were transmitting a worldview, a sense of the self. By learning these stories ancient peoples could find their own place in the world. The Bible is far more than an oral tradition, eventually written down, and passed from generation to generation. As we said above, the Bible stands out among all traditions, among all texts, among all stories because it is true.

The Bible is a unique story by a unique Author, God. And because it is God's story, it is true. And because it is true, it gives us a true account of the world and of our place in it. As we listen to the Bible's story, we begin to understand where we fit in and how the moments in our lives and the things around us fit together. We begin to make sense of our world and of our lives when we understand the story.

The Bible is a great story. It is a true story. It is the story that makes sense of us, of every moment, whether those moments are utterly confounding or seemingly insignificant.

THE MAKING OF A GOOD STORY

Stories tend to have a few things in common. A good story has a beginning, a middle, and an end. The biblical story begins at the beginning, *the beginning*, that is. We look around the world and we see everything: sky, land, flora and fauna, animals of all sorts. Where did all this come from? The Bible starts us off with a most fascinating scene. There is darkness and deep and formlessness and void. Into all of this primordial chaos, God speaks and brings to life all that there is.

The deep, the waters, are separated and the heavens and then the land appear, bringing form to formlessness. The land, the air, and the seas are then filled with creatures, filling what once was void. This is some beginning.

The middle is worth looking at as well. It is a series of twists and turns, unexpected setbacks, and unexpected advances. And then there's the end. The classic story always has the happy ending, especially if it's a Disney movie. Everyone comes out a winner—except the really bad guys. Sometimes, though, the endings are not so happy, leaving things unresolved and unsolved.

Back in the nineties there was a critically acclaimed television series called *Homicide: Life on the Street*, following the lives and work of homicide detectives in the city of Baltimore. Critics hailed it for its reality, for its rawness. Unlike most cop shows, this one tended not to glamorize police work. Scenes of bored cops reading the paper in the break room hadn't made the cut in previous television cop shows. While critics hailed it, the series languished in ratings and the network eventually pulled the plug, canceling the series. Apparently, the city of Baltimore didn't find the series all that flattering, either.

One of the reasons people think this show tanked among a watching public is that a number of the cases in the episodes went unsolved. They didn't always catch the bad guy, sometimes never even getting so much as a suspect. No resolution, no solution, no happy ending. *Homicide: Life on the Street* was sort of like the line from C. S. Lewis's Narnia, "always winter and never Christmas." Unlike some of the episodes on *Homicide,* the biblical story has a happy ending. That happy ending, however, doesn't come cheaply or easily.

A good structure of a beginning, middle, and end makes for a good story. But it's not all you need. The plot makes the story. The better the plot, the better the story. In fact, the better the plot, the more interesting the characters in the story.

We've all been disappointed by a movie that has one of our favorite actors. We watch in anticipation only to find that, no matter how good our favorite actor is, the story is awful, really bad—predictable plots, lack of imagination, no twists, bad dialog. On the case of the DVD or on the Netflix website, there should be a movie cop, instructing us, "Move along, folks, there's nothing to see here."

TRACING THE PLOTLINE

The story of the Bible has not just any plot, but the best plotline of them all. In fact, its plotline of fall and redemption becomes the template for any good story, any good novel, and any good movie. The biblical plot involves "trouble in paradise," that is, the original trouble in the original Paradise. It also involves a resolution, a solution. We could actually identify four elements to the biblical plot. They are:

Creation

Fall

Redemption

Restoration

These follow the flow of the biblical narrative itself. We start off with creation in Genesis 1–2. This is a world of harmony, of perfect peace. But it doesn't last long. Right on the heels of the creation account comes the fall in Genesis 3. The fall, shattering the peace that reigned over the created order, becomes one long and thick strand, winding its way through Scripture and on through history right up to the present day.

But the fall is not the only reality governing biblical and post-biblical history; it's not the only strand of the plotline. Also in Genesis 3, right alongside the fall of humanity into sin and the curse, God offers the promise of redemption in the seed. Like the fall, the plotline of redemption, the plotline of the seed of the woman who will undo the effects of sin, also runs through biblical history. The plotline of redemption culminates in the four gospels and the birth, life, death, and resurrection of Jesus Christ. The plotline of redemption carries right on through to the present day.

The Old Testament books anticipate the coming of redemption against the backdrop of creation and fall. The four Gospels speak of the Redeemer and his work of redemption. Acts and the New Testament Epistles unpack the work of Christ for the church, explaining the meaning of his work and his words for the very first generation of Christians and for us.

Like the hub of a wheel, redemption is at the center of the story and fans out like spokes through the biblical narrative.

26

The individual stories, those spokes on the wheel, catch our eye and as we read them, they lead us right to Christ and his work on the cross.

That leaves one last book, Revelation, and one last piece to the plotline of the story, restoration. Christ's death and resurrection set in motion the beginning of the end. Theologians call this the already/not yet, or the even more sophisticated-sounding term, *realized eschatology*. These terms refer to the kingdom, the eternal kingdom that the prophets of the Old Testament couldn't stop talking about. Amos talks about a future time, after peeling off a thickly layered judgment, when the "plowman shall overtake the reaper and the treader of grapes him who sows the seed" (Amos 9:13).

Imagine, the crops are so heavy, so abundant, that they can't even be harvested before it's time to plow up the field for the next planting. Imagine, so many grapes that they can't even be treaded. That's a lot of wine—or grape juice, if you prefer.

Ezekiel envisions a massive temple all decked out and filled with the glory of God. It takes him eight long chapters just to describe it (Ezekiel 40–48). These and many, many other prophecies are all about the future kingdom, the visible and unmitigated, unrivaled, unsurpassed reign of God over all things.

When Christ rose again from the dead and ascended into heaven, he set in motion the kingdom. Building on a score of Old Testament prophecies, Jesus is the Davidic King and his kingdom has started. But there is much more to his kingdom that has not started. That's why theologians call this the already/not yet. Jesus is *already* ruling as King; the kingdom has come, but only initially. There is more reign to come, more kingdom to come. That's the *not yet* part.

Many use the term *eschatology* to refer to this subject, a word taken from the Greek which means the study of last things or the study of the end times. We'll use the term *restoration*, and even the term *consummation*, to speak of this fourth and final piece to the plotline of the biblical story.

ON TO THE STORY

So we move from creation, then next to the fall, then next to redemption, and then finally to the restoration and consummation. We go from Genesis 1 to Revelation 22, from the eternity before time, through all of human history, and on to eternity future. That's one big story. Now you can see why breaking it down into creation, fall, redemption, and restoration helps you get a handle on it.

These four pieces to the plotline pop up all over the pages of Scripture. Getting the big picture of this biblical narrative helps make sense of all the various details in Scripture, as well as all the details of theology. And, as we'll see, it even helps make sense of your life. In fact, apart from this story nothing makes much sense at all.

This is just a quick picture of each of the four stops of the plotline. The next four chapters treat each one with a much more in-depth treatment. Time to move out to the deep end.

(2)

IT WAS GOOD: CREATION

This is my Father's world;
He shines in all that's fair.
—Maltbie D. Babcock

For the beauty of the earth, for the glory of the skies,
For the love from which our birth over and around us lies.
Lord of all, to Thee we raise,
this our hymn of grateful praise.
—Folliot S. Pierpoint

THIS PAST SUMMER I was helping my father-in-law chop up and split a rather large beech tree that had fallen in his woods. The tree seemed to take half the woods with it, cutting down scrub trees and masses of briars as it fell, and opening a clearing into some far reaches where he had never been.

When we walked back the sixty or so feet of the length of the tree we found that its trunk had been rooted right up against a natural spring, which let out a cool stream filled with moss-covered rocks and flanked by rows of ferns. I had never seen anything so green—especially since I had never been to Ireland. It was pristine, the water crystal clear and pure.

PARADISE

For a moment I had a brief glimpse of what Adam and Eve experienced every day, everywhere they turned—the greenest green, the bluest blue, the clearest clear, the purest pure. This was not just in some isolated spot, but everywhere they looked. Of course, they experienced far more than breathtaking scenery.

Adam and Eve together experienced perfect harmony with the creation they saw and worked in and tended. They witnessed perfect harmony within the creation itself. And, best of all, they experienced perfect harmony with the Creator. We know from Genesis 3 that Adam and Eve enjoyed perfect harmony with God, enjoying times of walking with him in the cool of the evening after the day's work and in those precious twilight hours as the sun began to set. This was paradise.

THE GOD OF CREATION

As you read the creation narrative in the opening chapters of Genesis, a few things come to the surface. Creation confronts three problems: formlessness, void or emptiness, and darkness (Gen. 1:2). Genesis uses water and the deep to describe this pretemporal, pre-creation world. Other ancient traditions also spoke of the deep, of the seas, this way. The seas were viewed as chaos, full of dark mysteries, full of threat. The ancients would look to their gods to battle the deep, or even to battle darkness, in hopes that through the struggle somehow the gods could subdue these forces.

German scholars came up with the term *chaoskampf* to describe this motif (or to be hard-core German about it, *kaoskampf*). Rivaling stories of intergalactic battles from the best of sci-fi, these ancient Near Eastern creation stories viewed the beginning of life in the universe as a fight, a struggle (*kampf*) against chaos among rather fantastically described creatures and gods.

The biblical account of creation both connects with these stories, by using some similar language, and also breaks with them at the same time. It breaks with them by offering a unique deity, one who does not struggle with the deep or the darkness, or fight the chaos. God merely speaks and it is subdued. No struggle, no fight. No *chaoskampf*. God speaks and he subdues.

What we have here is an utterly unique creation account and an utterly unique God. The Bible is not one story among others, not one creation fable alongside other fables of the ancient Egyptians or Babylonians. The creation account is framed in such a way as to communicate something specific and deliberate to its original audience and to us. And that something has everything to do with God.

The early creeds of the church stressed this idea of God as Creator. "I believe in God the Father Almighty," begins the Apostles' Creed, "Maker of heaven and earth." Creation shows God's power, God's might. Creation even points to God's existence, his creation standing as a constant testimony to his presence in the world. God is *present*. God is here. And God is powerful.

That testimony to God in the creation, the testimony of the stars and the mountains, even of the deserts, finds expression in words in the creation account in Genesis. When ancient readers engaged that word in the opening chapters of Genesis, they saw immediately the goodness and greatness of God. They saw him as unique. As they kept reading the narrative, they would also find that this unique God strikes out in an entirely unique way to establish a relationship with his creatures, with humanity. God is not far off. He is not distant and uninterested. God longs to be with us, with his treasured creation.

THE GLORY OF CREATION

Everything about the biblical account of the creation of humanity is remarkable. First, God crowned his creation with his ultimate handiwork, humanity, whom he created in his image as male and female. We see this not only in Genesis 1–2, but also in Psalm 8, in David's hymn of reflection on the glory of creation and the far greater glory of the Creator. There David declares of human beings that God has "crowned him with glory and honor" (Ps. 8:5).

God made all sorts of magnificent creatures, from the great whale and giant squid in the oceans, to the agile jaguar or the stately lion. Despite all of their amazing features, which we admire from safe distances at a zoo, all the creatures of the world lack something compared to us. They all seem so small in comparison to us, even the 100-foot, 200-ton blue whale. Not one of these creatures is made in the image of God. God made humanity his crowning achievement.

A second thing that comes to the surface also concerns us. God gave us everything we need to fulfill our purpose of bearing his image, subduing and having dominion over the earth, and obeying him. First, he conquered the problem of formlessness, void, and darkness. But he did far more than just subdue the deep, creating a most variegated and complex world. And he made Adam and Eve with the capacity to rule over it, evidenced first in Adam's naming of the animals.

Parents know this ritual all too well. Whether it's a frog, a bug, or a turtle, or any other creature that gets within your kid's grasp, it has to be named. Naming it signifies ownership, even rule over it. No longer free to hop along at will, the captured frog, placed in the cardboard box along with a stone and some grass clippings, now answers to the child—at least until it, whatever it's named, can hop over the side and make its escape. God placed Adam and Eve in the garden, and he gave them the wherewithal to do what he commanded them to do.

I spent the summer of 1989 in Hungary, working at a Christian camp. The camp was owned by the government and had been used to train youth in the communist way. With the end of the Cold War and the collapse of the Soviet Union's hold over Eastern European nations like Hungary, the camp no longer had the purpose it once did. The new government, anxious to put its past behind it, leased the property to a Christian organization to run a new kind of summer camp.

I have many memories from that summer, including the memory of the disappearance of my laundry, which had been hanging out to dry. My American T-shirts and my shorts now belonged to a band of gypsies, encamped not too far from the property. It was particularly memorable to see my Coca-Cola T-shirt from time to time around the village. And I also remember a bucket and a well-worn sponge.

Much of the camp had fallen into disarray, the cabins for campers in desperate need of repair. Workers came in to shore up weak spots and to paint. I was tasked with coming along behind and cleaning up. Handed the aforementioned well-worn sponge and bucket, I was also given access to a sink. A bucket and sponge, however, seemed to be not quite up to the task of removing bits of dried, splattered concrete and paint spills. I did not have what I needed to do what needed to be done. We have all been there.

But not Adam and Eve. When God put them in the garden and commanded them to have dominion over it, he gave them all they needed to do the job. They were equipped.

THE BEAUTY OF CREATION

So far we have seen that humanity stands alone and stands out as God's crowning achievement. We have also seen that God gave Adam and Eve all that they needed to do what had to be done. We also see one more thing rise to the surface in these chapters of the creation account. It comes in Genesis 2:9. This verse, tucked away in the second retelling of the creation, often gets overlooked. Here we are told that God made every tree that is both good for food and pleasing to the eye.

This little verse expresses two purposes. The first is that of utility. We have in creation the resources that we need to survive, to live. We have food and, especially in the case of Adam and Eve, good water. But there is a second purpose here. The creation is beautiful, a source of pleasure, something to be enjoyed.

God made this world as a place of habitation for human beings. As creatures in it, we have what we need to survive, even thrive. But God gave us more. He gave us a world we can enjoy. God provided for our pleasure.

Writing many centuries after the creation, Jonathan Edwards, a New England colonial minister of some fame, picked up on this theme of God's providing for our pleasure. Edwards was conducting an experiment regarding the so-called flying spider. He figured out the spider wasn't exactly flying. Instead, the spider released a web that initially was lighter than air. This piece of web would float along, attach to a far-off tree limb, and then harden. The spider then retracted the web. Hence, the spider "flew."

Now Edwards maintained that this particular species of eight-legged creature "flew" in order to get food. He also surmised, and this was in an age where scientific enquiry was a bit different from that of our age, that the spider also enjoyed himself as he propelled through the air from tree to tree. He concluded that God is so gracious that he provides not only for the sustenance of insects, but he provides for their enjoyment, too.[1] To paraphrase Christ's comment about sparrows from the Gospels: Are not we far more valuable to God than the flying spider?

God not only provides for our needs through creation, he also provides for our pleasure and our enjoyment. Too often we fail to let our eyes see the beauty that God has put around us. I read once of a painter who spent two years making a series of paintings of a particular tree at different times in different seasons under different conditions. The locals barely ever took notice of the tree until the artist forced them to notice it. Then they saw it; then they enjoyed it. Artists have a way of seeing beauty in what the rest of us take for granted, what the rest of us barely notice. We could all likely do well by developing an artist's eye.

As we read through the creation account we see at least these three ideas we have been discussing so far:

- God made us in his image, setting us apart from his creation; we are his crowning achievement.
- God equipped Adam and Eve with everything they needed to do what had to be done.
- God made a creation that is pleasing to the eye; he made a beautiful world for our enjoyment and for our pleasure.

We'll come to see that there's quite a wrinkle in this creation, brought about by the fall—stay tuned for the next chapter. But this is still our "Father's world." These three ideas may not be true for us to the degree that they were true for Adam and Eve before the fall. But it's a matter of degree, not a matter of all or nothing. We still remain creatures in God's image set apart from the rest of creation. We still remain equipped, though seriously marred by sin.

The world, despite the ravages of sin and the toll of generations of sinners upon it, is still beautiful, still a source of pleasure, still to be enjoyed. And all human beings, although deeply marred by sin, still reflect the image of their Creator. There remains a dignity and sanctity of human life. Recovering this doctrine of creation and all that it entails seems especially crucial to us today. To make this point a bit sharper, consider a parable, the parable of Timothy and his boredom.

THE BORED LIFE ISN'T WORTH LIVING

Most of the time, Timothy was bored. As a kid he seemed to care little for the things around him and even less for the people around him. Timothy's mom would send him out to play and he would be bored. He didn't explore. He didn't imagine. He didn't even look up at the birds and the clouds or down at the caterpillars and spiders (he is a boy). At school, his mind thought about play. At play, he could only think of everything he didn't have to play with, only thinking of all the toys he didn't have.

Eventually Timothy became an adult and carried his boredom with him. At his job, he could only think of play and fun. When he wasn't working and out trying to have fun, he could only think of everything he didn't have. On his way home from work he didn't look at the clouds in the sky. He missed sunrises, and he shrugged at sunsets. Timothy yawned through his childhood, school, work, family, and friends. Timothy yawned through life and right on into death.

Let the reader understand the meaning of the parable. Timothy had no sense of wonder whatsoever. Timothy squandered a precious gift from God, the gift of life, by caring little for God's gift of creation. Timothy and his boredom is not just a parable, however. And, sadly, Timothy's not alone.

A few decades back, Neil Postman wrote a scathing critique of American culture, indicting us all for, as the title has it, *Amusing Ourselves to Death.* Now, a few decades later after billions of dollars and countless hours spent in the full-throttled pursuit of pleasure, we have amused ourselves right into boredom. We are a culture adrift in a ship of boredom. What's tragic is that we are actually in this ship while we are floating in a sea of wonder.

To try another metaphor, if the American Medical Association were to label boredom a disease, we would have to declare an epidemic. And our kids would be at dangerously high levels of risk for catching it. We are bombarded with the spectacular on an hourly if not minute-by-minute basis. What's left for us to have? What's left for us to experience? I don't know about you, but I'm glad the expression "been there, done that" has passed its shelf life. The expression, while it was alive, nevertheless captured this malaise.

Boredom begets a loss of a sense of wonder. Our loss of a sense of wonder begets a loss of appreciation. And our loss of appreciation begets a loss of gratitude—quite a downward spiral.

SAYING THANK YOU

Read through the Old Testament and you find that God simply wants us to be grateful, to be quick to sing his praises, and to tell our Heavenly Father, who showers us with good gifts, thank you. When Augustine, the towering saint in the early church, wrote his *Confessions,* he started by declaring that God had made him, and that God made him for the express purpose of entering into a relationship with him. "You have made us for yourself and we are restless," Augustine says, "until we find our rest in you."[2] But Augustine did not seek God; instead he wandered far off.

All this comes in the first chapter or book of the *Confessions*. Before he leaves the first book, however, Augustine draws one significant conclusion. Augustine tells us that all God required of him was simply to acknowledge him and then give him praise, express gratitude, and say thank you. But this, Augustine would not do. Nine books and many years later, with many twists and winds in the path, Augustine finally said thank you. When God gripped his heart and turned him around, Augustine's first response was to offer up praise to God.

Augustine's retelling of his early life and ingratitude reflects the opening chapter of Paul's epistle to the Romans. There Paul declares that we failed to acknowledge God, turning to the creation and the creatures over and against the Creator (Rom. 1:28). Paul also tells us that we "did not honor him as God or *give thanks* to him" (Rom. 1:21).

This problem of ingratitude was not just in the first century of Paul or in the fourth century of Augustine. The Old Testament prophets almost incessantly indict Israel for two big sins: idolatry and ingratitude. The two actually go together, just as acknowledging God (instead of turning to the creation) and giving thanks to God go together in Romans 1. Idolatry is the displacement of God, the turning to a cheap substitute.

When we see ingratitude on par with idolatry we should be shocked. God had ransomed his people, brought them out of Egypt, and put them in the Promised Land. Yet, they refused to acknowledge him, turning to idols instead; and they refused to offer him thanks, offering up muted voices of ungrateful hearts.

Ingratitude extends beyond the centuries of Old Testament Israel. God has placed us as humans in his world. More often than not, we offer up grumblings of ingratitude instead of grateful praises from thankful hearts. God made us and he has made us for himself. He wants us to acknowledge him and to express our gratitude. Instead, we put our hands in our pockets, shrug our shoulders, let out a yawn, and walk off. Perhaps, it's true. Since we've lost our sense of wonder, we have forgotten how to say thank you.

Embracing the doctrine of creation is the antidote to boredom. When we realize that God made us, that God made everything, life is set in a whole new light. How can we yawn at what God made? When we acknowledge God as Creator of all things, we regain our sense of wonder, we regain our sense of appreciation, and we regain our sense of gratitude. We say thank you. We stop yawning through life.

THE SOCIAL LIFE: CREATED FOR RELATIONSHIP

So far we have learned from creation that humanity is God's crowning achievement, that God provided a perfect and pleasing environment, and that a little gratitude goes a long way. There's one more piece, and that is that God created us as social beings.

The Swiss theologian, Karl Barth (pronounced *Bart*, the *h* being silent), picked up something in the creation account that many seemed to have missed. There's a great deal of discussion swirling about the topic of the image of God. We'll delve into this more later, but at this point it's helpful to bring in Karl Barth and his take on the image. Barth noticed that the image of God is explained in the next phrase as "male and female."

Look at the poetic structure of the lines from Genesis 1:27:

In the image of God he created him;
male and female he created them.

39

This leads Barth to say that the image of God is gender. Now at this point many, misunderstanding Barth, dismiss him outright. His idea is quite complex, though, so it may be worthwhile to hear him out. When he says gender, he means relationship. The image as male and female represents the one that needs the other, the one that finds its counterpart in the other. If we flip over to Genesis 2:24, we see that in marriage the two, male and female, become one flesh.

Barth isn't putting down being single here, and he isn't saying that only married people are truly people. What he is saying is that human beings are social creatures not as a luxury, but as a necessity. For Barth, the image of God means relationship, and relationship is essential to being human. Relationships or being in relationship is what defines us. We were made for each other.

God not only created us to have fellowship with each other, but he also created us to have fellowship with him. Let's think this through. God did not create us because he had to. He doesn't need us. Unlike us—his human creatures who need each other, God needs no one or no thing. He's complete in himself.

Here's one for the quiz. Theologians of the Middle Ages spoke of the *aseity* of God. This English word literally means, from its Latin roots, that God completely exists *from himself,* that he is not dependent on anything for his existence. He does not need anything or anyone. The aseity of God means that he lacks absolutely nothing at all. He is utterly complete in himself.

So if he doesn't need us, why did he create us? The answer is he wanted us. While God doesn't need us, he is a social creature himself. This bumps into the doctrine of the Trinity, that God is three persons in one substance or essence. God did not become a Trinity when he created the world. God was and is eternally a triune being. In the early church, some theologians called this idea the "social Trinity." This means that God is a social being, worshiping and glorifying and enjoying himself.

We have to be careful not to express this in a way that sounds as if we're talking about three Gods. The doctrine of the Trinity is rather tricky, and we have to be very cautious in our expression of it. But, within the boundaries laid down for us in Scripture and in the creeds, we can and we must say that God as a Trinitarian being is a social being.

The crucial question is: What does this idea of the social Trinity have to do with us? The short answer is, everything. God created us because he wanted and wants us to participate in him, to participate in this triune fellowship. He made Adam and Eve so that they could be brought into the perfect union of fellowship that already existed within the triune Godhead.

Picture it this way: God's love and even enjoyment of himself was so large, so great, that it spilled out into the creation of the world, resulting in a widening of that circle, of that perfect union. God's crowning creature, humanity, who was created in his very image, would be brought into the divine fellowship. God created us because he wanted us. God created us for relationship with him and for relationship with each other.

There's a reason psychologists label antisocial behavior a pathology. We were not created for isolation and exclusion. We were created for relationship. We are social beings.

CONCLUSION

Creation is the opening act of the history of the world, of the Bible, and of God's grand story. As we look into the creation account in Genesis 1–2 and the biblical reflections on creation in the rest of Scripture, we learn that humanity plays a crucial role in God's plan and enjoys a special place in the created order. We are created in God's image, creatures of dignity and even, using David's word from Psalm 8, of honor.

God has provided us his world, stocked full of that which we need and also filled with that which passes beyond sheer necessity. God has made a beautiful world for us to enjoy. We also learn that God made us for each other and for himself. And all he asks is that we look around in wonder and offer him gratitude.

These are the opening scenes of the story. In many ways this is like most stories. The characters are enjoying themselves; all is right with the world. They're even happy. But as you watch you have that uneasy feeling that somewhere offstage lurks the antagonist; somewhere off the horizon looms the problem that's going to disrupt all the harmony and good times.

So it is with the biblical story. We look upon Adam and Eve with a certain uneasiness. We watch them in the garden, tending it. We watch them playfully, lovingly smile at each other. We watch them walk with God in the cool of the evening. And as we watch them, we want to shout at them, to warn them. We want to warn them, because we know all too well what's coming next.

3

TROUBLE IN PARADISE: FALL

Man, the world ain't supposed to work like this.
Maybe you don't know that, but this ain't the way it's
supposed to be.
—Mac in *Grand Canyon,* Cited in Cornelius
Plantinga, *Not the Way It's Supposed to Be*

Something is rotten in the state of Denmark.
—Shakespeare, *Hamlet*

ONLY C. S. LEWIS could get away with a quote like this:
"Don't talk damned nonsense." It comes from his wonderful book
that has introduced so many to the Christian faith, *Mere Christianity*. Let me put the quote in context.

Lewis plays out a conversation for us between a pantheist and
a Christian. The pantheist, one who believes that all is god and

consequently that all is good, when "confronted with cancer or a slum" will say, "If you could only see it from the divine point of view, you would realise that this also is God." Lewis says in reply, nonsense.

Then Lewis counters with the Christian view. Christianity, Lewis contends, "thinks God made the world—that space and time, heat and cold, and all the colours and tastes, and all the animals and vegetables, are things that God 'made up out of his head' as a man makes up a story. But it also thinks a great many things have gone wrong with the world that God made and that God insists, and insists very loudly, on our putting them right again."

You'll have to wait a few chapters until we get to the putting-things-right part of the quote. This chapter concerns the part of Lewis's quote that deals with the great many things gone wrong. In these sage words, Lewis reminds us of the famous quote from Shakespeare's *Hamlet,* "Something is rotten in the state of Denmark." All was not right in the castle at Elsinore. And young Hamlet knew it.

It is the Christian view that all is not right with the world, not just with the state of Denmark. Take heart, Danes, we're all in this together. This Christian view, in fact, is the only view that makes sense of the horrific things that happen in our world—the things we see on the news and the things we try to shield ourselves from experiencing firsthand. To think that all is just fine is, as Lewis said, damned nonsense.

WHEN THE WHEELS FELL OFF THE WAGON

Cornelius Plantinga Jr., has written one of the best books on the worst topic of all, sin. He defines sin as the violation, vandalization, scandalization, disruption, and even perversion of *shalom.*[1] Now to fully grasp this, we start with shalom. The word literally means "peace." But as Plantinga explores the term, he unpacks a great deal from it.

Shalom is what may very well have been written over the garden in Eden. There was perfect peace, perfect harmony, perfect wholeness all around. Shalom marked the relationship between God and Adam and Eve. It marked the relationship between Adam and Eve—imagine no bickering, no fighting, no petty arguments. Shalom marked the relationship Adam and Eve had with the creation, and it marked the relationships within the creation to itself. Over it all hung one word: shalom.

Then Adam and Eve disobeyed God, inviting the new reality of sin into the pristine and pure garden. And when sin came in, it brought all sorts of ugliness with it. It brought along death and contention and strife and thorns and pain. It disrupted shalom, all levels of the shalom that governed life. The new normal of life after the fall would be disharmony, disunion.

The curse that God lays upon Adam and Eve and creation in Genesis 3:14–19 bears all this out. Read through those verses and with every line a wedge is driven further and further between Adam and Eve, between them and God, and even between them and the ground itself. This world that was shalom was and is now fallen. The image of God in humanity was and is now marred. It is now, as Plantinga's book is titled, *Not the Way It's Supposed to Be*.

This is the point of the story at which we gasp in horror. Not so much because of what we just saw, but because we know this to be all too true of our own lives and our own experience. We, as part of the human race, have that nagging suspicion that something isn't right, that things are off. It is, indeed, not the way it's supposed to be.

Dietrich Bonhoeffer once said that not only is this a fallen world, but it is a falling-fallen world. By that he meant that sin has a life of its own. Like a parasite, it grows and grows, greedily feeding off of its host.

SIN CROUCHES AT THE DOOR

When Adam and Eve fell, they turned on each other. Their once-perfect relationship was now spoiled by their ratting each other out, their blaming each other, and their pointing of fingers from one to the other. Adam may have turned on Eve, but Cain slew Abel. Sin has an exponential effect, plunging us into a downward spiral.

In Genesis 4:7 there is another one of those verses tucked away and often overlooked. God tells Cain that "sin is crouching at the door." Like a fierce enemy-in-waiting, sin stands ready to pounce. And it does. It catches an all-too-willing Cain in its grip and wreaks havoc on the first family. Imagine Eve's sadness on hearing the news. The events started in the garden of Eden were working themselves out in a most inhuman way. But this is now the new normal.

Coming to grips with the fall is a crucial element to grasping the story. It is the fall that sets the stage for redemption. Without a proper, which means low, view of the human heart, we can't have a proper, which means high, view of the cross and what Christ did there. It not only sets the stage for redemption, but it also gives a clear-eyed view of ourselves. We live in a culture that seems rather content to ignore our true condition. We have anesthetized ourselves to the raw effects of sin. We have done this largely by distracting ourselves. Coming to grips with the fall gets us past the static and distortion of the distractions.

NUMBED TO SLEEP

George Orwell entitled his doomsday book of the future *1984*. But 1984 came and went. That fact was not lost on social critic Neil Postman. In 1985, he published his now classic book, *Amusing Ourselves to Death*. Here's what he has to say in the foreword of his book. I quote it at length so you can get its full force:

We were keeping our eye on 1984. When the year came and the prophecy didn't, thoughtful Americans sang softly in praise of themselves. The roots of liberal democracy had held. Wherever else the terror had happened, we, at least, had not been visited by Orwellian nightmares.

But we had forgotten that alongside of Orwell's dark vision, there was another—slightly older, slightly less well known, equally chilling: Aldous Huxley's *Brave New World*. Contrary to common belief even among the educated, Huxley and Orwell did not prophesy the same thing. Orwell warns that we will be overcome by an externally imposed oppression. But in Huxley's vision, no Big Brother is required to deprive people of their autonomy, maturity and history. As he saw it, people will come to love their oppression, to adore the technologies that undo their capacities to think.

What Orwell feared were those who would ban books. What Huxley feared was that there would be no reason to ban a book, for there would be no one who wanted to read one. Orwell feared those who would deprive us of information. Huxley feared those who would give us so much that we would be reduced to passivity and egoism. Orwell feared that the truth would be concealed from us. Huxley feared the truth would be drowned in a sea of irrelevance. Orwell feared we would become a captive culture. Huxley feared we would become a trivial culture, preoccupied with some equivalent of the feelies, the orgy porgy, and the centrifugal bumblepuppy. As Huxley remarked in *Brave New World Revisited*, the civil libertarians and rationalists who are ever on the alert to oppose tyranny "failed to take into account man's almost infinite appetite for distractions." In *1984*, Huxley added, people are controlled by inflicting pain. In *Brave New World*, they are controlled by inflicting pleasure. In short, Orwell feared that what we hate will ruin us. Huxley feared that what we love will ruin us.

This book is about the possibility that Huxley, not Orwell, was right.[2]

From this lengthy quote, two things should be noted. First, consider the phrase from Aldous Huxley that we have an "almost infinite appetite for distraction." Second, consider Postman's observation that Huxley's futuristic view has won out over Orwell's, at least as far as our current age is concerned. We are, in our ceaseless quest to be distracted, destroyed by that which we think brings us freedom and pleasure. We are, in other words, our own worst enemy.

Now consider this. How much further has our entertainment culture plunged itself into the relentless pursuit of distraction since 1985? There is much static and distortion, distracting us and keeping us from coming to grips with who we really are because of the fall and sin.

It's easy to point the finger elsewhere, especially if we wave our pointed fingers at the broad sweep of culture "out there." The reality is each of us as individuals have been influenced by this slumping toward distraction and numbness toward sin. The fall reminds us how tragic sin really is. The fall reminds us how tragic our own sinful hearts and our own sin really are.

DAVID SMILING

Our church bulletin comes in a kids' edition, and each week the cover portrays artwork of a child in the church. I told our one son, six at the time, he should draw something for the cover. A few minutes later he handed me his drawing. I looked at it, showed it to my wife, and we promptly decided we would not submit it for publication on the cover of the kids' edition of the church bulletin.

He had drawn scenes from the life of David, scenes from the incident with Bathsheba. The first scene had the two rooftops, with David, the stick figure with the crown, looking at a stick figure Bathsheba. The roofs, I must say, looked remarkably like ancient Israelite roofs. The next scene has Uriah dying in battle, a hunched-over stick figure with spear in hand. My six-year-old got the story. He got it quite well, actually. We weren't exactly sure, though, how well it would go over on our church's bulletin cover.

There's more to the first scene he drew, the one of David looking at Bathsheba. In it, my six-year-old son has David smiling. Again, my son got the story, got it quite well. Sin is pleasurable to us because in our sinful nature, in our fallen state, we are bound to it. Let me clarify this—sin seems to be pleasurable for us because we don't know any better.

At the fall, we lost our way. We lost our orientation. We had been oriented toward God. At the fall, our orientation shifted off of God and onto the self and onto sin. Martin Luther once said we were made for God and made to live "toward God." But at the fall we came under the disease of *incurvitas*, a Latin word, which sounds like something a dentist might call a bad tooth. No, the word has nothing to do with a dental disease. The word means "curved in," or "self-ward." Instead of being "toward God," we are "toward our own selves," says Luther. With our twisted orientation, we have a twisted view of what brings us pleasure and what brings us fulfillment.

But here's the rub. We think satisfying the selfish and sinful desires brings pleasure. It doesn't. It only brings pain. The Rolling Stones might be right after all. We just "can't get no satisfaction." But we try, and we try, and we try.

BOUND TO SIN

Paul sheds a great deal of light on this in Romans 1. We already looked at the first chapter of this magisterial epistle in our discussion of creation. We need to return to these verses to understand sin and the fall.

In our previous look at Romans 1, we saw how we responded to God as creator. We would not honor God and we failed to give him thanks (Rom. 1:18–21). We preferred the creation and creatures, including our own selves, over the Creator. So God "gave us up" to what we wanted.

Paul uses this expression, "God gave them up," three times in Romans 1:24–28. And each time the expression sets the stage for a further twist in our downward spiral away from God and a further twist straight into the clutches of our own sin. By the end of the chapter, Paul throws out a list of sins that we can barely read through without blushing. Such was the effect of Adam and Eve's transgression in the garden. The compounding effect of sin comes to collect its prize.

That prize is the wrath of God. Judgment is something we would rather overlook. We cry out for justice almost constantly. We should be careful, though, in what we wish for. Justice, true justice, requires that each and every one of us faces a reckoning for our rebellion against God. Paul at one time calls us "children of wrath" (Eph. 2:3). As we look to the suffering and death of Christ on the cross we see the penalty for sin. We see the full weight of God's holy wrath and perfect justice bearing down.

We see this even before Christ's trial and crucifixion. We see it at Gethsemane (Matt. 26:36–46). The setting of Christ's agonizing prayer and struggle with the Father before he goes to the cross is not mere coincidence. Gethsemane is a garden. It was in a garden that humanity turned on God, rebelling against him and bringing about the penalty and misery of death and separation. And it is in a garden that the God-man, the incarnate Lord, would intensely face the prospect of bearing the cup of God's wrath.

The gospel makes sense only in light of the fall. Paul starts with our sin—he *must* start with our sin, in his portrayal of the gospel. We have become numb to what we are capable of and what we are guilty of through our long intake of the anesthesia of distraction. Reading Romans 1 and coming to grips with the fall offers the perfect antidote.

LIMITATIONS

Coming to grips with the fall entails a few things, as we have seen. One more thing it entails hasn't been considered yet. In our culture of limitless potential, in our culture where the promise of technology offers freedom from limits, we must come face-to-face with the idea of limitation.

When God placed Adam and Eve in the gardens he gave them a limit. They could eat of the fruit of any tree they wanted, except for one. They could not eat the fruit of the tree of the knowledge of good and evil (Gen. 2:17). Such a limitation was nothing compared with the limitations brought on Adam and Eve as the consequence of the fall. Now Adam and Eve and all of us would be limited in our work, would be limited in our relationship to each other, and would be limited in our relationship to God. Even the garden itself would be "off limits" to Adam and Eve.

Think this through. Adam and Eve departed from the perfect ability to work and produce, the perfect ability to get along with each other, and the perfect ability to fellowship with God. All of that was left behind when they were expelled from the garden. There is irony here. By refusing to accept a single limitation, not eating of that particular fruit, Adam and Eve plunged themselves and all of humanity into a world of limitations. The human heart continues to crave, to desire satisfaction. We want what we can't have. And in our sin we go after it all the more.

Bathsheba was David's forbidden fruit. But David couldn't accept the single fact that he couldn't have her. He refused to accept his limitation. And that sin plunged David and his posterity into a further downward spiral of death and misery. The words from Genesis 2:17 echo through history: "*The day that you eat of it you shall surely die.*"

READING SIN

While the chapter of the fall is the least welcome chapter of the grand story of the Bible, it is nevertheless a necessary one. The reality of the fallen world is that we are bound to sin, not free to be the men and women God created us to be. The reality of the fallen world is that, while sin looks pleasurable, it pays out in misery and sorrow. The reality of the fallen world is that we have limitations. The reality of the fallen world is that we are all under the wrath of God, and our judgment day is coming.

Our culture, or any culture for that matter, seems to run from each of these maxims as fast and as far as we can. We run to this distraction and to the next and to the next. We have entertained ourselves into a comfortable numbness. These cultural pressures assert themselves on us, even those of us who have been redeemed. We, too, come under the influence of the anesthesia of distraction from sin's true nature and sin's true consequence. Reading about the fall, being confronted with the fall, coming to grips with the fall—that is the essential and absolutely necessary corrective to these cultural pressures that cause us to stumble and drift.

Sometimes we want to wince at what we read in Scripture. We see Jephthah, so foolish in his rashness in offering his own daughter as a sacrifice. We see Lot committing incest with both of his daughters. We see Israel's beloved king plotting to take another man's wife and then plotting to take that man's life. We see the despicable things a zealous Paul does in what he thinks to be the service of God as he relentlessly tracks down Christians. We want to wince, and rightly so.

These things are not there to titillate us. This isn't R-rated entertainment. What we find in this ugly part of the story, the chapter of the fall, is who we truly are. These stories of the fall and of sin and its consequences are there to call us out of our numbness and to bring us to grips with the reality of the fall and sin and the human condition. Reading about the fall, though unpleasant, is actually life giving.

A scene from Harper Lee's *To Kill a Mockingbird* illustrates this well. Scout Finch, the six-year-old narrator of the story had just returned from a day at the courthouse with her brother, Jem. They had snuck into the balcony to watch their father, Atticus Finch, defend the falsely accused black Tom Robinson of the rape of white Mayella Ewell. Later that night, when the three members of the Finch family had made it home, Scout and Jem's aunt rebuked her brother Atticus for allowing them to hear part of the trial. Atticus shot back, "It's just as much Maycomb County as missionary teas."[3]

We prefer the genteel. We all want to live in a village right out of a Thomas Kinkade painting. But the fall is real. The impact of the fall, in all of its ugliness and bitterness, is real, too. All too real.

God in his graciousness does not whitewash the human condition and the consequence of sin. In his Word, he has revealed who we truly are, what we are capable of, and what we face as a consequence. Don't look away from these parts of the story. Instead, read them and be humbled and cry out for mercy. And then praise the gracious God of our salvation.

CONCLUSION

As we close out Genesis 2 we see that all is good, very good. But as we see it we hold our collective breath because we know what comes next in the story. We know what happens in Genesis 3. In all of our talk of the fall and the effects of Genesis 3, we skipped over something, though. It is something that is all too important.

Amid all of this curse and bad news, there is a lace of promise. There is hope. What Adam did at the fall, Christ will undo in the next chapter of the story, the chapter of redemption.

4

UNTO US, A CHILD: REDEMPTION

Most action is based on redemption and revenge, and
that's a formula. *Moby Dick* was formula. It's how you
get to the conclusion that makes it interesting.
—Sylvester Stallone

We have peace with God through our Lord Jesus Christ.
—Paul

MY FRIEND WALT MUELLER drew my attention to a
photograph and a story in *Christianity Today*. The photo is of a
young man on the seat of a bike, while a woman sits sidesaddle.
The man in the picture is Marc Sahabo, a Hutu from Rwanda.
The woman is Felicita Mukabakunda, a Tutsi from Rwanda. Their

picture accompanied an article written by Mark Moring, who met the pair while on a missions trip in Rwanda. In the article he tells their story.

REDEMPTION IN RWANDA

Before the genocide that ravaged Rwanda, the two had been neighbors; their extended families had been friends. During the genocide Marc Sahabo personally murdered fifteen Tutsis, among them the father and uncle of Felicita Mukabakunda. While she and her husband and children were hiding in a marsh, she overheard Marc Sahabo and a machete-wielding mob of bloodthirsty and power-crazed Hutus vowing to kill her and her whole family. She even heard Marc and the others talk of how they would gang rape her first.

Felicita Mukabakunda and her family managed to escape their would-be killers, living as refugees in a camp until the long, dark night of Rwanda passed. Marc, who had fled to Tanzania, was sent to a Rwandan prison for his crimes, being released in 2003. He attended a reconciliation workshop sponsored by Rwanda Partners, one of the ministries working to bring peace and healing to Rwanda. Through the workshop, Sahabo testifies that, "My heart was changed by Jesus." And he began to seek forgiveness from his victims.

His journey of confession and repentance led him straight to Felicita Mukabakunda. In the wake of the genocide, wounds still fresh, she had vowed that she would someday make Sahabo pay. But now he stood before her, then he kneeled, then he begged for her forgiveness. And she gave it. They became, as they claim, "best friends," and took to the bike to travel the villages of Rwanda, telling their story of repentance and forgiveness, their story of redemption, their story of reconciliation.

There is no way to explain the picture of Marc Sahabo and Felicita Mukabakunda together on that bike apart from Christ's work of redemption on the cross. Mark Moring quotes Theo Mushinzimana, of Seattle-based Rwanda Partners, "Any reconciliation in Rwanda is a result of a biblical process that brings perpetrators and victims together at the foot of the cross."

THE CROSS AT THE CENTER

There is no way to understand this story apart from the truth of the story of the Bible, the profound truth of redemption. There is no way to understand this story apart from the grand story and the grand center of the story, Christ and his work for us on the cross. The story of Marc Sahabo and Felicita Mukabakunda actually illustrates the entire grand narrative itself. They, before the genocide, were friends, neighbors. Then came that horrible moment as the Hutus rose to power and unleashed the wickedness of the soul upon neighbor, upon friend, even upon family members.

We do not need to look any further than the atrocities of the genocides of the twentieth century, like that in Rwanda, to prove the reality of the fall, the reality of sin, the reality of evil. Even the most secular voice of culture finds that evil is the only word capable of describing these events. But as real as sin and the fall is, redemption and forgiveness is, too. And because redemption and forgiveness is real we can have hope; we can have peace.

PEACE WITH GOD: JUSTIFICATION

The first two and a half chapters of Romans sketch out our sin and the consequences. Paul sums up his teaching by stringing together a series of Old Testament quotes (Rom. 3:10–18). The upshot is this—we are sinful and there's nothing we can do about it. As Paul says, "None is righteous, no, not one" (Rom. 3:10).

Then we come to Romans 3:21 and the words *but now*. This sets the stage for the solution. The righteousness of God is not something we earn, because we can't. It's something we're given because of what Christ has done for us. The theological term here is justification, one of the most important doctrines of our faith and one of the most important words we could know.

The doctrine of justification teaches us that Christ in his obedience, his perfect obedience both in his life and in his death on the cross, accomplished for us what we could not. Christ satisfied the holy and just demands of God as the penalty for our sin. Paul puts it this way in 2 Corinthians 5:21, "For our sake he made him to be sin who knew no sin, so that in him we might become the righteousness of God."

Returning to Romans, Paul sets forth our sinful state from 1:18 on through to 3:20. Then Paul introduces the theme of justification from 3:21 on through to the end of chapter 5. At the first verse of chapter 5 Paul tells us something that should be emblazoned on our hearts and minds and ever before us. "Since we have been justified by faith," Paul declares, "we have peace with God." This justification came, as Paul expresses it, "through our Lord Jesus Christ" (Rom. 5:1). We, sinful, fallen creatures who ran off in our own rebellion, now have peace with the just and holy and righteous Creator of all things.

We saw in the last chapter on the fall how sin marred God's world and the shalom that defined it and gloriously ruled over it. Now, because of what Christ has done on the cross, shalom is restored. As soon as Paul says "peace with God," he goes on to say three times "we rejoice" (Rom. 5:2, 3, 11). We have peace with God. Our only response can be an overflowing of joy.

PEACE WITH GOD: RECONCILIATION

Peace with God not only relates to the theological term *justification*, but it also relates to the theological term *reconciliation*. Paul also says in this fifth chapter of Romans that, through the work of Christ, "we have now received reconciliation." To best understand reconciliation we need to look at its opposite, alienation. To be alienated means to be cut off, to be estranged, to be a stranger in a strange land. Paul deals with this concept in Ephesians 2 and Colossians 1. Alienation is one of the heinous consequences of the fall. Right after Adam and Eve sinned, when they heard God calling out to them, they hid from him.

What a different day that was than every day that preceded it. On every other day, when God called to them, they ran to him and walked with him, fellowshiping together in the cool of the evening. But not on this horrific day. On this day they ran away from him, and they hid.

That begins humanity's alienation from God. When Adam turned on Eve and Cain slew Abel—that began humanity's alienation from each other. We are, in the words of philosopher Thomas Hobbes from his book *Leviathan*, in a "war of all against all." We are all at odds with God. We are too tragically often at war with each other—both literally and figuratively speaking. We are even, it seems at times, at war within our own selves. That is alienation.

Through Christ's work on the cross we are reconciled; we are brought back into relationship with God. We can even be restored to each other. Paul expressed this numerous times in terms of the Jew and Gentile division, a division that ran sharp in the first century. Read more about Paul on reconciliation in 2 Corinthians 5:11–21, Ephesians 2:11–22, and Colossians 1:15–23. In these texts Paul offers a great summary of alienation and reconciliation.

59

Reconciliation slams on the brakes and throws us into a 180. We who were far off from God were brought near. The dividing walls of our hostility toward one another have been torn down. And we even have peace with our own selves. That is reconciliation. And that's what it means to have peace with God. Again, our only response should be that of overflowing joy. We have peace with God. We also rejoice. We also rejoice. We also rejoice.

THE SEED TO COME: TRACING THE PLOTLINE OF REDEMPTION

The theological ideas of redemption, justification, and reconciliation find a significant place in the writings of Paul. Some, like Martin Luther of the past, saw redemption and justification right at the heart of the Apostle's thought and writings. But Paul isn't the only one in Scripture who has something to say about redemption.

This is the central theme of the Bible. It is the good news of the plotline. It is the happy ending to the tragedy that began in Eden and has coursed through human history. We can get a handle on the plotline of redemption by tracing the biblical teaching of the promised seed to come, the one who would provide for and be our redemption. To trace the plotline of the seed we go back to the beginning.

In Genesis 3:15, there is the promise of the offspring of the woman who will crush the head of the Serpent. In Galatians 3:16, Paul identifies this seed as Christ. Going from Genesis 3 to Galatians 3 is quite a trip. If we take a step back, we'll see how this promise, first given in Genesis 3:15, finds its realization in Christ.

We know that the seed to come, the one that would deliver humanity from this plight of sin and death and separation from God, was not Cain or Abel—Adam and Eve's first offspring. We also know it wasn't any of the long list of people coming at us in the genealogy of Genesis 5. All of these people died.

When Abraham came on the scene in Genesis 11, God trucked out the promise from back in chapter 3 (read Genesis 12–15, especially 12:1–3). But alas, Abraham himself wasn't the seed and neither was his son Isaac, or his other son Ishmael. Then we come to Moses. He makes for a good candidate and does deliver God's people, but he too falls short. Then there's Saul. It's soon rather obvious that he won't work.

Then there's David. Now he stands a chance. In 2 Samuel 7, through the prophet Nathan, God brings out the promise of the seed again (2 Sam. 7:8–17). Then David dies. There is also a related problem of some of the things David did while he was alive. So could it be Solomon? Could he be the seed?

We need to put ourselves into the context of the Old Testament, knowing the promise of the seed to come, the deliverer of humanity. If we do, we will soon find ourselves chiming in with David, "How long, O Lord?" We will find ourselves in a state of expectation, of hoping that with each successive generation there will be the one we've been waiting for. When we do put ourselves into the context, we can understand the overwhelming joy of an old man named Simeon who held vigil by the temple doors. When Mary and Joseph brought the infant Christ to the temple, Simeon grabbed him out of Mary's arms, held him up, and cried out to God, "For my eyes have seen your salvation" (Luke 2:22–35).

Next came an old woman named Anna. She, too, made a proclamation concerning this child, telling all those who were waiting for redemption that they could now give thanks to God (Luke 2:36–38). There's also Mary's song, known as the Magnificat, and the prophecy of Zechariah, John the Baptist's father, both in Luke 1 and both praising God for his merciful work of salvation that has now come through the seed, Jesus. Hope fulfilled; promise delivered. Even the genealogies of Christ in the gospels make it a point to connect all of the dots, telling us, collectively, that Jesus is the son of David, the son of Abraham, the son of Adam (Matt. 1:1 and Luke 3:38).

Then we get to Paul. Paul, though he is quite complex, has a way of simplifying things. Paul expresses humanity as breaking down into two groups, defining these two groups as either "in Adam" or "in Christ" (Rom. 5:12–21 and 1 Cor. 15:12–49). We are all in Adam; we are all his offspring. Keep going back, back, back, back, and we all bump into Adam at the root of our family tree. It takes nothing more to be in the club known as "in Adam" than to be born. And being in that club means, as Paul describes it, slavery, death, and alienation—the utter and complete absence of shalom. But then comes the seed of Adam, the one who restores shalom. Paul puts it clearly in 1 Corinthians 15:22: "For as in Adam all die, so also in Christ shall all be made alive." In Adam there is nothing but slavery and bondage, guilt and remorse, condemnation and death. In Christ there is nothing but freedom and liberty, forgiveness and peace, justification and life.

THE SEED: INFANT SON, INFINITE SAVIOR

What's amazing about this story of redemption is the Redeemer. In this case, the Redeemer, the main character, is entirely and utterly unique. He both identifies with us and is distinct from us. He is the God-man. Isn't it interesting that our deliverer comes from us? Isn't it interesting that our deliverer was born of a woman, born under the law (Gal. 4:4)? He was born and lived and suffered and laughed and cried.

He was fully human, the offspring of the woman. The word *incarnation* literally means "en-fleshed." Make no mistake about it, Christ was fully human. Yet, he was also God.

Britain's great preacher Charles Haddon Spurgeon once said:

Infinite, and an infant.

Eternal, and yet born of a woman.

Almighty, and yet hanging on a woman's breast.

Supporting a universe, and yet needing to be carried in a mother's arms.

King of angels, and yet the reputed son of Joseph.

Heir of all things, and yet the carpenter's despised son.

When we look at the work of Christ for us and for our salvation, we begin to understand why the Redeemer, the seed who would come to deliver humanity from the clutches of sin, had to be the God-man. He had to be human to identify with us, the offending party. We were the ones who sinned against God. Yet, he needed to make a worthy sacrifice, an acceptable sacrifice for sin.

We understand the level of the need of this sacrifice when we see the level of the offense. Adam and all his posterity, which includes us, sinned against the holy and true God who made us. That's an incredible offense. Christ in his humanity identified with the offending party. In his deity he provided the satisfactory sacrifice, his atoning blood of infinite worth.

TEARING DOWN WALLS

As we saw above, Paul uses a number of terms to describe Christ's work on the cross, including *redemption*, *atonement*, *justification*, and *reconciliation*. All of these are both packed and beautiful terms.

It's hard to believe, but nearly all of my current students were born after Ronald Reagan left the presidency. They missed out on the eighties and the Reagan era altogether. As with most presidents, historians and critics are divided on interpreting him and his legacy. But most if not all agree that he was a great communicator. He knew how to turn a phrase.

One of those many phrases of his was bellowed from the concrete structure snaking its way through Berlin, Germany. "Mr. Gorbachev," he declared, speaking to the prime minister of the former Soviet Union, "tear down this wall." And with the collapse of the Berlin Wall and the demise of the power of the Soviet Union over the Eastern Bloc nations came the end of the Cold War.

As Jesus died on the cross for us and in our place he tore down the walls that divided and alienated us. Through his death he reconciled us to God. We have peace with God through the work of the seed.

THE REDEEMED COMMUNITY

But there's more. Christ was not reconciling individuals to individual lives of service to God. Christ was hammering out a new community. Back to Bonhoeffer: "Christianity means community in Jesus Christ and through Jesus Christ. . . .We belong to one another."[1] As the story of the fall is really the story of the fall of us, so the story of redemption is the story of the redemption of us, of God's people. This highlights what is central to God's plan and purpose—the church.

One of the things that plagues us as Americans is our entrenched notion of individualism. African and Asian Christians are quite helpful in bringing this to the surface. In those cultures community, or the tribe or the clan or the extended family, is the essential and defining element of human identity. But we Americans like our freedom and individual identity. We can sometimes let this spill over into the way we read the Bible or the way we think about theology.

When we think of sin, we can always and only think of our sins. When we think of redemption, we can always and only think of our redemption. This seems to particularly plague American evangelicals who reduce redemption to a personal relationship with Jesus Christ. Bonhoeffer, however, was right. Read the New Testament and you trip over the metaphor. The church is a body, a symbiotic and collective whole. (See 1 Cor. 12:12–30 for a concentrated treatment of the body metaphor.)

The poet John Donne put it this way, "No one is an island."[2] How true that is when it comes to the redeemed community. Christ's work of redemption paves the way for the establishment of that crucial piece of God's plan, the church. You can read about it in Acts 2 and 3 and 4 and 5 and, well you get the picture.

In other words, when we talk about redemption, we also need to be talking about the church. When we talk about what it means to be a Christian, we have to be talking about our Christian life in the new redeemed community of the church. No one is an island. The Liverpool Football Club (and that's the round kind of football) has a great motto that applies to the church: "You'll never walk alone."

READING REDEMPTION

Redemption reverses all that was set in motion at the fall. Redemption is at the heart of the story. In fact, *redemption is the story*. The Greek word *gospel* literally means good news. We get the word *evangel*, or *evangelism* from it. This is the good news for a lost and fallen world. This is the good news that we need to hear.

There's not much of the Bible that does not contribute in some way or another to redemption. As we read the story of the Bible, we are continually presented with new and richer and deeper dimensions of redemption. We sometimes live in a world of wave upon wave of bad news. Returning to the good news of the gospel can be just what we need.

In 1739, Jonathan Edwards preached a long series of sermons, thirty sermons in all, on one verse. Well, to be exact, half of a verse. He chose the text of Isaiah 51:8b, "But my righteousness will be forever, and my salvation to all generations." He titled the series, "The History of the Work of Redemption."

Of course, Edwards only used this text as a jumping off point. Throughout the thirty sermons, he roamed freely over the pages of the Bible. But he kept coming back to the idea in this text. The one thing that holds all of the centuries together, the one thing that holds all of Scripture together, is God's grand design of redemption.

Edwards was teaching his congregation, and anyone else who takes the time to read the sermons, how to read the story of history and how to read the story of their individual lives. He was doing this by teaching them, and us, how to read the Bible. When we read the Bible, we read history; we even read the story of our own lives in light of and under the umbrella of redemption.

One recent book on philosophy asks, "Does the center hold?" In other words, in light of our postmodern times, there are many who wonder if there even is a center—that which gives meaning to everything. And if there is such a center, does it or can it hold? Does it hold everything together? The good news is that there is a center. And what's more, the center, the grand narrative of redemption, holds.

Going back to that singular verse, Isaiah 51:8 offers an even more persuasive argument for viewing all of life and history and the Bible from the center, from redemption. In the first half of the verse, the prophet observes, "For the moth will eat them up like a garment, and the worm will eat them like wool." In the context, Isaiah is referring to the wicked, and the wicked taunt the people of God for believing in him. To counter this, Isaiah points to their transient nature. They will pass. They will come to an end. But God's salvation will not. It lasts and lasts.

One way we could look at this is to see how easily we are dismayed and misled by appearances. We look at the world around us, or we look at the events unfolding in our own lives, and we think righteousness is being overtaken by the wicked. Based on appearances, it looks at times as if we're losing.

The reality is we are not. God's will and God's kingdom will prevail—all appearances to the contrary. The reality of the situation, of any and all situations, is "My righteousness will be forever, and my salvation to all generations" (Isa. 51:8b).

In these sermons on this prophetic text that echoes throughout the whole of the Bible, Edwards is teaching us how to read. He's teaching us how to read the Bible, how to read history, how to read these early decades of the twenty-first century. And he's teaching us how to read the story of our lives. We'll never go wrong by reading it all through the prism of redemption.

Redemption paves the way for the last piece of the story, the final curtain, if you will. The forgiveness of sins, being justified, being reconciled to God, having peace with God is only the beginning of redemption. It is but the first act. The act that follows is quite something, too.

5

HOPE'S COMIN' ROUND THE BEND: RESTORATION

This world must not be prematurely written off.
—Dietrich Bonhoeffer, while in a Nazi prison

FROM WHAT MUSIC SCHOLARS and historians say, it's not a true story. I wish it were. In the wake of World War II, Remo Giazotto claimed to discover the tattered remains of a sonata composed by seventeenth-century Venetian composer Tomaso Albinoni. Giazotto gave the next dozen years of his life to reconstructing this almost lost masterpiece. It has since been recorded many times over.

But Albinoni didn't write it. There simply isn't enough evidence to sustain Giazotto's claim that the piece is an original Albinoni composition. That credit likely belongs to Giazotto all himself. He spent twelve years composing it, not reconstructing it. The name of the piece, however, has stuck. *Albinoni's Adagio has* been performed, recorded, and enjoyed all over the world. It has achieved near iconic status as a piece of music.

The reason we all wish this were a true story is that we all hope. We long to see good come of bad, we long to see the ruins rebuilt and restored. To rescue and resurrect a fallen masterpiece from among the bombed-out and burned-out ruins of a war-torn European city would be something. A single piece of music can have a powerful effect. It could remind us of our humanity, of beauty. It could be cause for hope. But, sadly, this is not the case with Albinoni's Adagio. That it is not authentic does not detract, however, from the beauty of the piece. It does not diminish the beauty of the story. And what's more, it does not deflate our hope.

DREAMS DEFFERED

One of the things we heard a lot when we began our parenting journey, among all of those sage nuggets of advice so freely offered, was that kids are resilient. They'll fall and they'll get back up. They have an uncanny knack for bouncing back. That nugget of advice, along with a few others, actually turned out to be true.

My wife and I were just far enough away that we could only watch as our then-two-year-old veered right into the path of our then-eight-year-old and his bike. Whack. Bike hit her. Boom. She went down. We gasped. The eight-year-old started to cry as he felt so badly. But the two-year-old, the victim of this driveway collision, stood up, brushed herself off, and went bouncing along.

Kids are resilient, indeed. Hope is resilient, too. But even hope has its limits.

Langston Hughes, the great twentieth-century African American poet, knew all too well of the limits of hope. Hughes found himself dislocated from his southern roots as part of the great migration of African Americans from the South to the cities of the North. Through his poetry and his writing, he was able to give voice to the unsettledness of a displaced generation. As Hughes saw things, though, his generation's experience was not unique. As he saw things, he and his generation stood in a long line of generations who lived unsettled lives, generations of African Americans who could only participate in the American dream from a distance.

Hughes asks in one of his poems, "What happens to a dream deferred?"[1] He goes on to explore unthinkable answers. Does it dry and shrivel up? Does it sink? Does it explode? For some, like the ones for whom Hughes was giving a voice, hope was running out. Hope's resilience can be tested.

When we face intractable situations, when we see the walls closing in, we need to have, we must have, hope. People put hope in all sorts of things, all sorts of things that can't ultimately bear the weight. People put hope in other people. People put hope in politics and politicians. People put hope in pensions and retirement plans. People put hope in things that can't deliver.

WHEN WISH-DREAMS DISAPPEAR

These misguided hopes soon veer into wish-dreams. And these dreams get deferred. I suspect one of the most tragic ways to live life is to live without hope. Friedrich Nietzsche wrote of the end of hope, the death of hope. He gave the world of philosophy a new *ism*, a new system of thought. Philosophers call it *nihilism*, which literally means *nothingism*.

In his day, Nietzsche was obscure, his work dismissed. But in the wake of the horrors, first of World War I and then especially of

71

World War II, a cadre of French writers and intellectuals seized upon Nietzsche's ideas. They brought the forgotten German philosopher a level of fame and popularity he never even came close to in his lifetime. They called themselves existentialists. They developed a philosophy that was quite dark, quite bleak.

One of them, Jean-Paul Sartre, once said the only question left for us now is, "Why *not* suicide?" Nietzsche and Sartre and the other existentialists rightly recognized that much of what people hope in disappoints. They saw futility and even absurdity when others could not. Like Dorothy, they had peeled back the curtain and saw an exasperated old man scurrying about at the controls of the wizard. Perhaps we reach the end of our humanity when we stop hoping.

Nietzsche and Sartre were right to not put their hope in the futile things that so many vainly rely upon. But they were wrong to stop looking for a place to put their hope. They offered up a true analysis of the problem. They had no idea, however, where to turn for the solution.

HOPE THAT IS REAL

As we turn to the Bible, we find the kind of hope that meets the *existential*, the urgent, needs of our lives. We find the kind of hope that meets the need to have the ruins restored. But much more, we find the kind of hope that is not a wish-dream. We find hope that is in fact a reality.

Biblical hope is a reality that has actually begun to occur, and it is a reality that, with the utmost of certainty, will fully occur in the age to come. No dreams deferred here. No hopes dashed. No hope-inspiring stories that turn out to be not true. No peeling back of the curtain only to find that everything we were counting on hinges upon a comedic old man pulling levers and pressing buttons.

CREATION GROANS

What Christ began at the cross will be brought to fruition. Our redemption, our salvation, is but the first act. The second act is the restoration of all things. As certain and true and sure as our forgiveness of sin, so certain and true and sure is the restoration of all things.

By connecting the restoration of all things to redemption, we gain a holistic perspective we sometimes lack. We tend to think of this life as one thing and the life to come as quite another. That kind of thinking can lead us to miss out on how God would have us live in this present moment. More on that in a little bit.

For now, let's keep this in mind: Christ began a good work in us at our salvation. That "good work" will be completed. No doubts, no uncertainties. We need to realize, as well, that the good work extends far beyond us as individuals. There is a cosmic dimension to this.

Paul speaks of the whole creation "groaning" for redemption in Romans 8:22. That good work has begun; it's happening now. And that good work will someday happen in full. No doubts, no uncertainties. In the Bible we find true hope. What's more, biblical hope is both strong and real enough to make a difference in this life.

WHAT WILL HEAVEN BE LIKE?

One of the most asked questions has to be the one asked by any sad child who just lost a pet. Will my dog or will my cat or will my fish be in heaven? I've received the question a few times myself. We want to know what heaven will be like. We want to know what we'll be doing there. While I have yet to find chapter and verse in the Bible concerning the presence of dogs in heaven, there is a definitive answer to what we will be doing in heaven. We do have chapter and verse for that one, Revelation 22:1–5, in fact. The short answer is we will enjoy fellowship with God and we will worship him. These verses from the last chapter of Scripture are so important, however, we need to linger over them for a while.

This passage offers a description that looks a lot like Genesis 1–2. There is a river and a tree of life and lots of fruit. It is a description of abundance, of order, of beauty. What's striking is the way Revelation 22 differs from Genesis, especially from chapter 3 of the first book.

THE BOOKENDS OF SCRIPTURE

Genesis 1–3 and Revelation 21–22 form the "bookends" of Scripture. Understanding how these bookends relate, and especially how what they each have to teach relates to us, is crucial to reading the story of the Bible. In the previous chapters we have spent some time with the first bookend. The final bookend is up now.

Revelation 22:3 declares plainly, "No longer will there be anything accursed." That ugly curse that trampled through the garden in Eden, leaving sin and misery in its destructive path, has been removed. It has been paid for in full by the Lamb, by Christ. And now there is no hiding from God, no separation. Instead, "They," meaning us as his redeemed community, "will see his face, and his name will be on their foreheads" (Rev. 22:4).

We are also told that night will be no more. God's glory, shining brightly, will be the all-encompassing reality. The clear light of day rules and night is fully extinguished. When Elie Wiesel wrote his Nobel Prize-winning memoir that recalled the horrors of his Holocaust experience in Nazi Germany, he simply titled it *Night*. That word encompassed his, then just a young boy, unimaginable experience. John the apostle, exiled at Patmos and bearing the scars of a lifetime of persecution, scrawls in the pen of an old and worn hand that night will be no more.

WORSHIP CHORUS

The first few verses of Revelation 22 also reveal what we will be doing for eternity. We will be worshiping God and reigning with him. We understand why we worship. We were created to worship, to be reflectors of God's glory back to him. First, Christ wipes out all of our and his enemies. Read Revelation chapters 6 through 20. Then he will establish the new heavens and the new earth ushering in the eternal state. Read Revelation 21. The final result? All those things that hindered perfect and pure worship will be fully and finally removed. We'll be so overwhelmed at this full and astonishing revelation of God that we will think of nothing but wanting to worship him. We can easily, if we think about it, understand the emphasis on worship.

Before the events of the end times, chronicled in Revelation 6–20, John peels back the skies to give us a glimpse of what's happening in heaven. An utterly overwhelming scene of visual images jumps off the page. There's a massive throne and a massive court, described as appearing like fine jewels.

Lightning flashes from the throne, flanked by flaming torches. Four creatures of wild description never cease to proclaim God as holy, and the twenty-four elders lie prostrate before the throne offering their praise. You can read it all in Revelation 4.

By the time we move to the end of Revelation 5, "myriads of myriads and thousands of thousands" of angels join the chorus of the four creatures and the twenty-four elders (Rev. 5:11). When John peels back the sky, we see but one thing, worship. Worship *is* the theme of heaven now; no wonder worship remains the theme of heaven for eternity.

APPROACHING THE END TIMES

I think it is important to start here when we think about heaven and the end times. Theologians use the word *eschatology* to speak of the end times. The Greek word *eschatos* means "last" or "the end," so eschatology is the study of end times.

Usually when we turn to the end times, we immediately bring up all the different views of end-time events. We talk about the timing of Christ's second coming; we talk of the rapture, of the tribulation. We draw up charts and we talk about secret keys to interpreting the prophetic passages of the Bible. We may even attend seminars to get the inside scoop.

By focusing on worship, the resounding biblical theme of life in heaven, we are both grounded and focused. Rather than devote our time to a lot of debate, we can be reminded of giving our time to devotion, to worship.

ESCAPISM OR UTOPIANISM? READING THE PROPHETS

Returning to the views of the end times, two conflicting positions came of age in the early twentieth century. The first hailed from the more liberal sector of Christendom and is known as post-millennialism.[2] This view is built entirely upon the optimism that reigned at the turn of the twentieth century. This view also drew heavily upon some thinking that arose in Germany.

In this view of liberal postmillennialism, the kingdom of God is interpreted as being wholly of this earth and wholly now. This is sometimes called *realized eschatology*, in that the events of the end times and the full and final coming of the kingdom are realized now.

Adherents of this view take Jesus' words, "The kingdom of heaven is in your midst," as teaching that the kingdom is here and it is now. There's no literal thousand years here. Instead, this view has the kingdom as a new, golden age that we are in here and now. We need to work, this view contends, to bring it to full fruition. This liberal postmillennialism also spawned the social gospel movement. This movement retranslated sin as social ills and consequently retranslated salvation as the coming of a social utopia in which the evils of famine and poverty and oppression are wiped out.

In opposition to this liberal postmillennialism arose premillennialism and dispensationalism. Whole books have been written on these topics. This current book is not one of them. But it is important to see some of the emphases of this view.

Especially in the early decades of the twentieth century, this view tended toward the polar opposite of postmillennialism. Rather than seeing the kingdom as wholly now, this view tended to see the kingdom as wholly future. If postmillennialism can be labeled utopianism, some versions of dispensationalism and premillennialism can be labeled escapism.

A popular expression gets at this escapism quite well. The saying goes something like this, "Why polish the brass on a sinking ship?" It's a rhetorical question. The answer is, don't bother. This world is barreling forward to its judgment day. All that matters is to save souls and wait for the kingdom to come.

This escapist view doesn't exactly give someone a place to stand as they survey their life and work in the quest of finding meaning. All of those things are merely means to the end. In fact, all of those things are much more of a distraction and hindrance rather than a help.

A THIRD WAY?

There is a third way, though. A few decades ago, theologians started using the term already/not yet. This idea avoids the extremes of the kingdom as wholly already, or that of the kingdom as wholly not yet. This view sees a combination of the two.

Let's make this concept a bit clearer. When Christ came the first time and died on the cross and rose again, he began the work of rebuilding the ruins. When Christ comes back the second time, he will complete the work of restoration.

This third way offers some continuity between this world and the next. This third way also provides a place to stand from which we can survey our life and work and from which we can find meaning. This third way also allows for those who hold to different views of the end times, different views of the rapture and the millennium, to have something in common. This, too, needs clarification.

Rather than seeing distinct camps regarding views of the end times, the already/not yet stretches the different views out on a continuum. The "distinct camps" view can often lead to barriers and walls of divisions. It lends itself to stressing differences and keeps other views at arm's length.

The already/not yet allows for an area of agreement, while still acknowledging difference. The dispensationalist sees a lot that is "not yet," a lot of biblical events are in the future. The premillennialist sees less that is "not yet." The amillennialist sees more "already," more biblical material related to the kingdom that is in play. And the postmillennialist sees even more "already" and far less "not yet."

The continuum approach, as opposed to the discrete camps approach, allows for differences but also has room, more room, to see commonalities. And when we see commonalities, we're more prone to listen to and learn from each other, rather than talk to and talk past each other.

There is a far greater benefit to the already/not yet, however, than fostering and facilitating better communication among theological positions. The already/not yet throws us back into this life with purpose and meaning and vision and mission. Let me let Dietrich Bonhoeffer show us how.

SENDING US BACK TO LIFE

Dietrich Bonhoeffer offers some encouragement here, not to mention some level-headed thinking. In one of his many letters from his period of imprisonment that led to his martyrdom, he explored this idea of the kingdom of God and our work and life on earth. Being in prison gave him clarity of vision. We would be wise to listen.

He's comparing the difference between the Christian narrative of redemption and other stories of redemption, demonstrating both the unique and superior nature of the Christian account. What's important is what he says about redemption in relation to life and living in the world. Bonhoeffer calls this "worldly discipleship." Let's see what he means by listening in on his letter:

> The decisive factor is said to be that in Christianity the hope of resurrection is proclaimed, and that means the emergence of a genuine religion of redemption, the main emphasis now being on the far side of the boundary drawn by death. But it seems to me that this is just where the mistake and the danger lie. Redemption now means redemption from cares, distress, fears, and longings, from sin and death, in a better world beyond the grave.

At this point, though, Bonhoeffer asks, "But is this really the essential character of the proclamation of Christ in the gospels and by Paul?" He answers, "I should say it is not." He explains why, and in the process he shows what our future redemption, our hope of resurrection, has to do with life now:

The difference between the Christian hope of resurrection and the mythological hope is that the former sends a man back to his life on earth in a wholly new way which is even more sharply defined than it is in the Old Testament. The Christian, unlike the devotees of the redemption myths, has no last line of escape available from earthly tasks and difficulties into the eternal, but, like Christ himself ("My God, why hast thou forsaken me?"), he must drink the earthly cup to the dregs, and only in his doing so is the crucified and risen Lord with him, and he crucified and risen with Christ.

Bonhoeffer adds a gripping and decisive conclusion: "This world must not be prematurely written off."[3]

Let me put this succinctly. God didn't redeem us to have us pine away for heaven. He redeems us, and then he hurls us right into the world to be his disciples and to be his church, his body on earth.

If we use the doctrine of the resurrection, the future restoration, and eschatology, as a means to escape this world, we are *abusing* these doctrines. The future hope of restoration, not to mention the restoration itself, hurls us back to terra firma, planting our feet firmly on planet earth.

The final chapter of the narrative, the restoration, is not merely a hope for some far-off day. It's a hope that gives us a vision for this life.

THINKING ABOUT SOME TEXTS

Let's apply these things we have been talking about to some specific texts. The first one up is Amos 9. Amos is a prophet unlike the other prophets. In fact, he claims not to be a prophet and, just to drive home his point, claims that he's not even the son of a prophet (Amos 7:14). Instead, Amos tells us he's a farmer. And this farmer from the sleepy country town of Tekoa went to Samaria to deliver

God's message to God's wayward people. He cycles through a series of judgments on the surrounding nations—speeches sure to draw cheers from the crowd gathered around him from Samaria.

Then Amos points his prophetic finger at Samaria itself and, as we would expect, the crowd and even the king turn on him. Unrelenting, Amos presses on. As we reach the end of his book, we see two significant themes emerge—judgment and restoration.

The prophetic books remind us of the full-orbed character of God. While we tend to look to Scripture mainly to see what it teaches about us, we should be first asking what Scripture teaches us about God. (We'll develop this idea of asking about God first more fully in chapter 7.) Here in Amos 9, the prophet declares God's justice, God's wrath, and God's holiness right alongside God's mercy, grace, and love.

Amos 9:2–4 sounds like Psalm 139. But in Psalm 139, God's omnipresence, which means that God is everywhere present, offers us comfort. There's nowhere we could go where God isn't. He's in the deepest valley, and that is a great comfort. Here, God is on the highest mountain and in the deepest valley, and that should shoot fear right through God's enemies. Here's what the prophet has to say:

> If they dig into Sheol,
>   from there shall my hand take them;
> if they climb up to heaven,
>   from there I will bring them down.
> If they hide themselves on the top of Carmel,
>   from there I will search them out and take them;
> and if they hide from my sight at the bottom of the sea,
>   there I will command the serpent, and it shall bite them.
> And if they go into captivity before their enemies,
>   there I will command the sword, and it shall kill them;
> and I will fix my eyes upon them
>   for evil and not for good. (Amos 9:2–4)

The prophets are full of such messages of judgment. The prophets are also full of messages of hope and restoration and future blessing. So it is with Amos. Amos anticipates a coming day in which, the judgment having occurred, God's graciousness returns and his goodness flows even more deeply and widely than his wrath.

Amos uses the language of his craft, farming, to express God's blessing. The crops will be so plentiful that they won't even have the time to harvest them before it's time to plant again. My farmer neighbors can't even imagine such a thing. Here's the prophet once again:

> "Behold, the days are coming," declares the LORD,
>   "when the plowman shall overtake the reaper
>   and the treader of grapes him who sows the seed;
> the mountains shall drip sweet wine,
>   and all the hills shall flow with it.
> I will restore the fortunes of my people Israel,
>   and they shall rebuild the ruined cities and inhabit them;
> they shall plant vineyards and drink their wine,
>   and they shall make gardens and eat their fruit.
> I will plant them on their land,
>   and they shall never again be uprooted
>   out of the land that I have given them,"
>   says the LORD your God. (Amos 9:13–15)

These messages of hope spill out over the pages of the prophets. They have their share of gloom and doom, but they also have plenty to say about the good news of the future. This is the basis for hope.

As Francis Schaeffer once put it, *How should we then live* in light of these future realities of judgment and blessing?[4] Peter asks the question this way, "What sort of people ought you to be?" (2 Pet. 3:11). Peter answers his own question by reminding us that we need to live holy lives, we need to wait for God's timing and for his bringing all things to his sovereignly directed and determined end, and we need to "hasten" the coming of the Lord (2 Peter 3).

This last point informs us how we are to "wait." We should wait actively, not passively. We should be engaged, not idle. The vision of restoration is intended to encourage us. It is intended to encourage us in our fight here on earth.

This prophetic message also serves as an alarm bell. It should wake us up from our spiritual slumbers and laziness. It should also drive us to repentance. Daniel, a prophet himself, knew this well. In Daniel 9, Daniel faced the full reality of the consequences of Israel's sin, and it drove him to his knees in repentance. He records what happened next:

> Then I turned my face to the Lord God, seeking him by prayer and pleas for mercy with fasting and sackcloth and ashes. I prayed to the LORD my God and made confession, saying, "O Lord, the great and awesome God, who keeps covenant and steadfast love with those who love him and keep his commandments, we have sinned and done wrong and acted wickedly and rebelled, turning aside from your commandments and rules." (Dan. 9:3–5)

Reading the prophetic texts should have the same effect on us. It's very easy to see the prophet's bony finger pointing at others. It's quite another thing to see if it's pointed at us. Daniel goes on to confess, "We have not listened to your servants the prophets, who spoke in your name to our kings, our princes, and our fathers, and to all the people of the land" (Dan. 9:6). May we listen to the prophets.

As we listen to the prophets, we will hear what God intends for us. He intends to be fully and really with us, his people. He desires to walk in the cool of the evening with us, as he did with Adam and Eve, but without even the slightest hint of the possibility of sin getting in the way.

The prophet Ezekiel ends his lengthy tome with a description of a massive temple. This temple is unlike any other in Israel's past. This temple blows them all away. After running through a litany of measurements and descriptions, Ezekiel gets to the point of it all, declaring, "And the name of the city from that time on shall be, The Lord Is There" (Ezek. 48:35).

Revelation 21 echoes this declaration. The final victory of God and the full realization of God's presence with his people boils down to God being with us. In heaven, God is *there*, fully and gloriously present.

> And I saw the holy city, new Jerusalem, coming down out of heaven from God, prepared as a bride adorned for her husband. And I heard a loud voice from the throne saying, "Behold, the dwelling place of God is with man. He will dwell with them, and they will be his people, and God himself will be with them as their God. He will wipe away every tear from their eyes, and death shall be no more, neither shall there be mourning, nor crying, nor pain anymore, for the former things have passed away." (Rev. 21:2–4)

Like Ezekiel 48, Revelation 21 also offers a description of the city complete with measurements. This city is dazzling with a nearly outrageous description of its jewels. But what truly radiates this city is the glory of God (Rev. 21:11). And this city is our final home.

Don't miss something rather telling in this text, though. The elder John writes, "By its light will the nations walk, and the kings of the earth will bring their glory into it, and its gates will never be shut by day—and there will be no night there. They will bring into it the glory and the honor of the nations" (Rev. 21:24–26). That glory and honor is derivative. All of it is nothing more than one grand reflection of the glory of God. While we know the source of this glory of kings and nations to be God, the question remains as to when and how this "glory" comes to be. Surely it comes at our "glorification," the time when our bodies are fully transformed and made new.

But perhaps this glory also comes from our lives, our lives on earth in our bodies. It is here on earth that we are in the process of transformation, from one degree of glory to another (2 Cor. 3:18). That certainly gives us something to think about, and to live out, while we wait.

For now we know in part, and see in part, and even live in part (see 1 Cor. 13:8–12). When the day of the Lord comes, when he brings his work of redemption to full fruition, the part becomes whole, the partial reaches completion. Now we—our lives, our knowledge, our relationship with God, and our transformation to glory—are in process. As you read the prophetic texts of Scripture, don't forget to keep this big picture in mind. In fact, let's flesh out some questions that can help you in reading these sometimes perplexing and sometimes hotly debated texts.

SOME QUESTIONS TO TAKE WITH YOU

Again, one word of advice on jumping into prophetic texts—keep the big picture of hope in view. It's easy for us to get lost in the details. We are tempted to run down rabbit trails of trying to decipher minutiae and looking for some secret insight into the details. Is Ezekiel's "wheel within a wheel" some sort of UFO? Are the locusts in Revelation Huey helicopters of the US Air Force?

Remember the big-picture reason why God reveals the future to us. He wants us to know what will happen so that we can have a real and abiding hope. God wants us to know what will happen so that we will trust in him that despite appearances, he controls the future and we need to trust and rest in him. He wants us to know what will happen so that we will work until he comes.

As you journey through these prophetic passages of Scripture, you can easily lose your way. These questions serve as guideposts to help you navigate these texts. Begin with trying to capture the big picture of restoration, and then work from that solid ground to sorting through and understanding the details.

Questions for reading prophetic passages of Scripture:

- What does this passage teach about the grand narrative of creation, fall, redemption, and restoration?
- What does this passage specifically teach about the coming restoration of all things?
- What have I learned from this passage about the future that I can put into practice now?
- What do I need to change in my life based on what I have learned about the future?
- How does this passage offer a different perspective on life, as compared to the perspective offered by our surrounding culture?

HOPE'S COMIN' ROUND THE BEND

We started this chapter talking about hope. We have explored the various contours of the biblical teaching of the restoration of all things. We have traveled far and wide. But the one thing that we cannot lose sight of is hope. If the creation is about shalom, and if the fall is about the loss and fracturing of shalom, and if redemption is about the restoration of shalom and peace with God, then the restoration is about hope—the hope for things to come, that makes a difference in our lives now.

I visited Grafton, Wisconsin, one August and it was cold. Pennsylvania, my home state, tends toward a mild climate, but in August we have our hot and humid days. This particular August we had experienced quite a string of such days. My warmed-up and thinned-out blood wasn't ready for the coolness I hit in Wisconsin.

I was there for the Paramount Blues Festival. Grafton had been the home of the Paramount Recording Company in the 1920s and '30s. Paramount was quite successful at what was called "race records." These were recordings of Southern blues musicians, most of them coming from the hot and humid climes of the Mississippi Delta.

Paramount sent scouts into the Mississippi Delta and other Southern regions in search of talent. When they found some, they gave them a train ticket to Grafton. One such singer was Charlie Patton. Patton first went to Grafton in the winter of 1929. If it was cold in August, then I can only guess how cold Wisconsin was in the winter.

Patton was from a land where it breaks 100 degrees in the shade in the summer. He was a long way from home. Patton fared quite well in the Wisconsin winter, though, racking up twenty-eight recordings on that first visit. He went back to Grafton in 1930 to lay down four more recordings.

He was quite far from home, in a cold and foreign land. But when Charlie Patton got behind a microphone with guitar in hand, he was perfectly at home. It was providential that Patton went to Grafton. By 1934, at age forty-two, Patton would be dead. Those Paramount sides provide us with well over half of the songs he recorded.

In them he sings of loves lost and pains encountered, the typical stuff of good ol' blues. But he also speaks of hope. "Jesus is my dyin'-bed maker," Patton's gravelly voice rang out as the machines carved grooves on vinyl records. Patton's life, like those of most of those Mississippi Delta blues men-and-women, was hard.

Sharecropping on cotton plantations was not all that different from the slavery of the previous generations. Oppression tended to be the rule and not the exception. Death came often to this world.

The world of the Delta desperately needed hope. And that's exactly what Charlie Patton sang of.

He sang of redemption and hope in and to a world that needed to hear it. Don't be fooled by our buttoned-up culture. We only look as if we have it all together. The people you live by and work with only appear to have it made. They are desperate, too. They are quite blue, despite appearances. We, and the people we love and know, need hope, too.

REBUILDING THE RUINS

There is another chapter to the story of Albinoni's Adagio. In the early years of the 1990s, the Bosnian War ravaged Bosnia and Herzegovina. The capital city of Sarajevo was under siege from 1992 until 1996. Snipers camped out on the hills. Bombs left craters and piles of rubble where buildings once stood. The city nearly came to a stop.

People huddled at intersections. On their daily forages for bread and water they scurried about Sarajevo's streets, dreading the open and vulnerable spaces of intersections. Many fell victim to the bullets of snipers. One of the many bombs dropped on the city exploded on a group of people lined up outside a bakery hoping to get a loaf of bread when it opened its doors. All twenty-two were killed by the blast.

The next day Vedran Smajlovic came to the scene. He set up a chair and removed his cello from its case and began playing Albinoni's Adagio. He returned almost every day for the next twenty-two days. Each day he would set up his chair, situate his cello among the rubble, and play Albinoni's Adagio.

"The Cellist of Sarajevo," as he came to be called, also played at funerals and would hold solo concerts in bombed-out buildings. Before the war he was a member of the Sarajevo String Quartet, the

Sarajevo Philharmonic Orchestra, and the Sarajevo Opera, among others. These organizations played often. They made recordings. During the siege, the orchestra members, like the rest of the city residents, hid for their lives.

But Smajlovic would not be stopped. He stepped into the rubble, into the ruins, and he would play. As he played he brought beauty into a dark and ugly time. As he played he brought hope. He played in bombed-out craters where buildings once stood, reminding the people of Sarajevo that they had a past and providing them with hope that they would have a future.

There are two ways we can wait for the life to come. One way to wait is to be passive. We can sit among the ruins and wait to be airlifted out. Or we can wait actively. We can sit among the ruins and play the cello.

The end of the story is glorious. Read Revelation 22:1–6 and you'll see just how glorious it will be. There will be a river and abundance, a restoration of Eden. There will no longer be any curse. There will be no more tears. No sorrow, no sadness, no sickness, no sin. And right in the center of it all is the throne of God and the throne of the Lamb. We will look upon his face and we will worship him and there will be no end.

That is a vision we need. That is a vision that God in his graciousness has given to us. He has peeled back the future and has shown us all that is to come. It is a vision of the life to come that has everything to do with the life we live now.

THE STORY WITHIN A STORY: PETER, PAUL, AND MARY

Characters welcome.
–USA Network

WE GETS DANIEL FOR A REFERENCE

The Reverend C. H. Savage of Mt. Ararat Missionary Baptist Church in Coahoma County, Mississippi, put it like this: "We gets Daniel for a reference." Savage spoke those words to Alan Lomax, an ethnomusicologist hired by the Library of Congress to trek through the Mississippi Delta. Lomax's mission? To record some of America's richest treasure before it was lost for good, the treasure of the spirituals and sermons of the black congregations dotting the cotton plantations along the Mississippi River.

Savage led the church in singing for Lomax an old "holler" song, a call-and-response song, called "Rock Daniel." "I'm gonna tell my Lord," Savage shouts, to which the choir simply answers, "Daniel." Next line, "How you do me down here." And again, "Daniel." Next line, "Slippin'and slidin' in the streets." Then back to the first line, "I'm gonna tell my Lord."

At the end of the song, Lomax kept the tape rolling as he interviewed Savage. "What's this song about?" Lomax asked. These songs were often full of "code." They were sung by slaves who used these songs to communicate with each other and to express how they were really feeling. They were hiding their thoughts "in plain sight" through these encoded songs. So Lomax is curious as to what this song is really about.

Savage answers Lomax directly and profoundly: "We gets Daniel for a reference." They felt just like Daniel. They were taken from their homes and found themselves in the fiery furnace a long way from home. Someday they'll be "slippin' and slidin' in the streets," code for dancing in the streets of heaven. They'll be dancing because they'll be so happy. But for now, this side of glory, they need hope. And they find hope in Daniel. God stood by Daniel. God will stand by them. They gets Daniel for a reference.

This is precisely how we should be reading the Bible. We should be taking Daniel, and a host of others, as our reference. In fact, again and again as the grand story of the Bible unfolds, any number of characters walks onto the stage to tell their stories, stories that give us a snapshot of the big story of the creation, of the fall, of redemption, and of restoration. We gets Daniel and we gets a whole cast of characters besides.

A CAST OF CHARACTERS

From the time we first could read or were read to, we met intriguing, funny, and lovable characters. Maybe you first remember Winnie the

Pooh or Curious George or Mickey Mouse. We find ourselves drawn to these characters, a testament to the power of marketing. But if we weren't so cynical, we would also have to admit we are drawn to these characters by the power of their stories, by the way they make us laugh, by the way they help us begin to make sense of our world.

And let's not forget our favorite characters in that well-read section of the newspaper, the comic strips. Of the many who have held our attention over the decades, few stand out as much as that lovable loser, Charlie Brown.

You may well remember the drill. Lucy tees up the football and assures her friend Charlie Brown that she will in no wise pull that ball away just before he unleashes all the might he can muster for the kick. Now it does not seem to matter that on the previous umpteen times she's pulled the ball away at the precise moment.

Her powers of persuasion convince Charlie Brown she's sincere *this time*. So good ol' Chuck gives it a go. And, of course, she pulls the ball away. And, of course, Charlie Brown lands flat on his back. Good grief!

Characters make the story come alive. They give flesh and blood to the plotline. Characters hold our interest, intrigue us. Good characters, complex characters, keep us coming back for more.

Characters are one of the three elements that make up a good story. Whether a good novel or a good short story, you'll find all three of these elements at work. They are:

- Setting
- Plot
- Characters

These three may also be found in the story of the Bible.

First, there's the setting. For this, the grandest of all stories, we have the grandest of all settings—the universe. The Bible is set against the backdrop of the earth. There are plenty of instances where the setting is much more local, at places like Mt. Sinai, Jericho, the Jordan River, and Jerusalem.

Then there's the plot. The creation, fall, redemption, and restoration paradigm we've been tracing is the plot. The narrative holds the sixty-six books together. The narrative functions like the spine functions for us vertebrates. We've spent the last few chapters tracing out this plotline of creation, fall, redemption, and restoration.

The plot is abstract, a concept. Characters add flesh and bone and dimension. Characters bring the plot to life. What we see in the grand narrative of the Bible is actually a composite of narratives. Stories make up the story. These narratives tell the grand movement from creation to fall to redemption to restoration. And they do it through the lens of the lives of individuals.

WHY CHARLIE BROWN ALWAYS TRIES TO KICK THE BALL

Characters have much to contribute to the story. The characters bring the plot to life. And the Bible has a lot of them; the Bible is full of them. These characters come from every walk of life, have every conceivable past and character traits—and many have quite inconceivable pasts and traits. At times they surprise us. Other times they don't.

Literature professors like to speak of different kinds of characters. Two simple classifications used involve the labels *static* and *dynamic* characters. Static characters are the predictable ones. They always act a certain way. They never change; they never develop or grow.

The Pharisees and the Sadducees would win any award for being the supreme example of a static character in the Bible. The moment you see them mentioned in the Gospels, you know exactly what they're going to do and how they're going to respond to Jesus.

The pharaoh in the story of the Exodus, when confronted by Moses, acted the same way. He'd say that he would release Israel, and then just as quickly he'd change his mind. Every time he would do the same thing—on cue. The last time this particular pharaoh shows up in the story, this static character trait of his dearly costs him and the people he leads (Exodus 14).

Static characters don't develop; they don't change. They experience all sorts of things, come into contact with all sorts of stimuli, but all to no effect. They merrily roll along. They don't learn from their mistakes. Every time Lucy tees up the football, Charlie Brown gives it a go.

Dynamic characters, however, develop, change, and grow. Sometimes these dynamic characters are also referred to as *round characters* because they show dimension and complexity. You can predict how flat or static characters will act in the scene, but make no predictions about round, dynamic characters. They will surprise you. Just once we'd like to see Charlie Brown refuse an attempt to kick the ball after Lucy tees it up.

TRANSFORMATION—OF BIBLICAL PROPORTIONS

The most interesting of the dynamic characters in the narrative of the Bible are those gripped by its plotline. The most significant change any of us can undergo, the most significant development any of us can experience, is the change from death to life, the change from existing as an old creature under the domain of sin and the kingdom of darkness to thriving as a new creature under the glorious domain of Christ and the kingdom of light.

It is not, however, a change we bring about by our own strength or by grit and determination. The transformation that lasts only comes about by the work of the triune God. We are passive and God is active. As we discussed in the earlier chapter on redemption, dead people can't do anything, and that is how the Bible refers to us in our fallen state. We are dead in our sin (Romans 3). God, the triune God, works a miracle to bring us back to life.

God the Father elects us and sets out the plan of redemption. Christ the Son secures our redemption through his life, death, burial, and resurrection. The Holy Spirit applies that work to us. As Christ told Nicodemus, one of the many interesting characters we meet in John's Gospel, we must be born of the Holy Spirit. When we see people transformed as we read the pages of the Bible, we are seeing the work of God. That's real transformation, and those who have undergone such a transformation are round characters indeed. And the Bible is full of such characters and their miraculous stories, stories within The Story.

READING THEIR STORY, READING OUR STORY

We can take the Gospel of John, for example. Consider the characters we meet up with in the early chapters of John's Gospel. There are the disciples. There's John the Baptist. There are the embarrassed hosts of a wedding. There's a doting mother anxious to see her son reveal himself as the Messiah. And that's just the first two chapters. As we come to chapters 3 and 4 we meet two rather opposite folks.

You could not find more polar opposites than Nicodemus in John 3 and the unnamed woman at the well in John 4. Nicodemus was a man—in a culture where gender mattered a great deal. John refers to him as "a ruler of the Jews." As a Pharisee, he enjoyed rank and privilege and power. Nicodemus took the top rung on the social ladder in first-century Palestine.

And then there's the woman at the well. First, she was a woman—again, in a culture where gender mattered a great deal. Secondly, she was a Samaritan, a people disdained. And she was multiply divorced. John tells us that Jesus stopped by Jacob's well, on the outskirts of Sychar in Samaria, on "the sixth hour," making it high noon. This was not the time the women at the village went to the well. She, this unnamed woman, was there because she occupied the bottom rung of the social ladder in first-century Palestine.

As we move through John's Gospel, we meet more characters. Roman officials, the blind, the paralyzed, servant girls, mass crowds—they all enter the stage and take their parts as the story unfolds. I think John includes all of these characters, this wide variety of characters, for a reason. We, if we're paying attention, will recognize ourselves in one of these characters. By reading about them, we will be reading about ourselves. And just as they are confronted by Jesus, so, too, are we.

The Gospel of John makes a compelling case for the gospel. It has so many clear verses on the gospel message. It paints a crystal-clear portrait of the humanity and deity of Christ and of his work on the cross. Little wonder that hundreds of thousands, even millions, of copies of John's Gospel are distributed all over the world.

It doesn't hurt that John also offers us all of these characters. The gospel message doesn't get handed down in some abstraction in John. It gets handed down to a highly regarded Pharisee who comes to Jesus by night, to a disgraced woman at a well, to a collection of outcasts huddled by the pool of Bethesda, and to a nameless crowd of well over five thousand.

We begin to see ourselves in the pages of John's Gospel. Who among us can remember a time when you were not so bold and courageous and, instead, were ashamed of the gospel? Then we read of Peter being confronted by a servant girl and denying Christ (John 18:15–18).

Who among us has not at a desperate time and under desperate circumstances wondered where God was? We longed for his presence to be felt but couldn't quite sense the peace of his presence. Then we read of Martha, mourning the loss of her brother,

Lazarus, meeting with Jesus and simply telling him, "Lord, if you had been here" (John 11:21).

We read these stories of these ancient people and we begin to read about ourselves. This is not just a reading strategy for John's Gospel. It applies to the whole Bible. This grand narrative plays out in the lives of people. God gave us their stories.

PETER, PAUL, AND MARY

One of these great stories is the life of Paul. In addition to his many accomplishments as a musician, Johnny Cash also tried his hand at writing a novel. He wrote his novel on the life of Paul, calling it *Man in White*. Cash did his homework as he set about the project. He pored over the life of Paul and the writings of Paul, and he read the history books and the commentaries. In the introduction he recalls the several years of work he put into the novel, even offering a great line after reflecting on his use of commentaries. "I discovered," Cash quipped, "that the Bible can shed a lot of light on the commentaries."

Cash's homework paid off. He produced an engaging and informative take on the Apostle. Even Cash's title shows just how well he got Paul. *Man in White* is a reference to Christ, the one whom Paul persecuted, the one whom Paul met on the road to Damascus, and the one to whom and for whom Paul gave his life. Cash knew that the main character in the life of Paul was not Paul. It was Christ. It was Paul himself who said, "No longer I . . . but Christ." That is profoundly and comprehensively true.

While we tend to pay a lot of attention to Paul's writings, we often don't pay as much attention to Paul as a person. But an intriguing person he was. He was fiercely smart. There are probably just a handful of people who could match wits with Paul. He could make an airtight and persuasive argument. He was compelling.

He was also driven. We first meet Paul as he relentlessly pursues Christians, the People of the Way, as they were called. Then, after his miraculous transformation, he relentlessly pursues the ministry of the gospel. Starvation, beatings, malicious detractors, imprisonments, and even a shipwreck—nothing stopped Paul. Yet, by Paul's own accounting of things, all that he accomplished added up to zero. It was all Christ at work in him.

The same may be true of Peter. Peter was a dynamic character. That's an understatement. We might be better served to see Peter as being on a roller coaster: at one moment, he's drawing a sword on a Roman soldier and slicing his ear, mere centimeters away from a fatal strike. The next moment, he's cowering before a servant girl as he warms his hands over the fire.

All of us have been there. Maybe we haven't been in these particular places. I can say for certain that I have never swung a sword at anyone, much less a Roman soldier. But all of us have felt the frustration encountered when we see Christ attacked. Conversely, all of us remember times when we were too embarrassed to speak up for our faith. We carry the shame of being ashamed.

Peter, too, faced uncertainty. After Peter's betrayal of his master, and after Christ's death and burial, Peter sensed that he had come to the end of the line. The last three years had been remarkable. But now it was over and all Peter had left to do was to go back and try to reclaim the life he had left behind. With a defeated sense, Peter declares, "I am going fishing" (John 21:3). But then the resurrected Christ appeared and everything, including Peter, changed.

We should all find a great deal of comfort and caution in the life of Peter. He's there in the story playing a significant role as God's grand design and plan gets worked out. But he's also there in flesh and blood, showing us what God's grand design really means. In Peter, we see ourselves. In Peter's story, we see our story.

LET'S NOT FORGET MARY

And then there's Mary. The New Testament has a few Marys, but the one I have in mind is the one we Protestants don't spend enough time on. She's not to be worshiped, and she's not an aid to our praying. But she is a powerful example.

Mary, who had a rather common name, was a rather common young lady. Not from wealth, not from nobility, she nevertheless possessed remarkable qualities, not the least of which was her devotion to God, her unflinching faith and trust in God. Perhaps the most striking element of the story of Mary is the irony of the most extraordinary miracle occurring in such common and plain circumstances.

The incarnation, the event of God becoming human and setting into motion the grand design of redemption, occurred in a most humble context to a most humble person. And what do we learn? We learn of her courage, her faith. We learn of her love for God. But we also learn of how overwhelmed she was by it all. After the birth of Christ and the visit of the shepherds, "Mary treasured up all these things, pondering them in her heart" (Luke 2:19).

From Mary's story we learn of how the holy and eternal God uses earthy and common means, uses common people, to bring about his will. And we learn that the only possible response is to be humbled and overwhelmed. We learn that we can't let such things go unnoticed. But like George Eliot's Silas Marner, who gathered up his gold, we should gather up all of the treasures of God's extraordinary dealings in our lives, and we should ponder in our hearts all that God does through us and for us. Mary pondered all of these things in her heart.

Besides Peter, Paul, and Mary, the Bible is full of characters, all with stories to tell. These characters are not mere props in the story. They're not wallpaper. They bring the grand story of creation, fall, redemption, and restoration to life.

HOW TO READ THE STORIES

What I'm suggesting here is that we focus on these characters and their stories in our reading of Scripture. We need to read the Bible in light of the people, real people, we find in its pages. On the surface, they appear different from us. But only on the surface. We, in fact, have much in common with these ancient people.

Let's use a far-out example to prove the point. I have hardly anything in common with the ancient Israelite widow Naomi. But only on the surface. I find Naomi's story to be profoundly compelling, and I have written of it elsewhere.[1] She fits this idea of being the story within the story perfectly.

Let me explain. When we first come to Naomi, she is in a bad strait. It's the time of the judges in Israel's history, a low point in Israel's life, and there's a famine in the land, which spells disaster in any times but especially in ancient times. So she and her husband leave Israel with their sons. And things go from bad to worse. Her husband dies, her sons die, leaving her only with foreign daughters-in-law—true liabilities and not assets.

So she returns home and the women of the village come out to meet her. "Is this Naomi?" they ask. She tells them not to call her Naomi, which means pleasant, but to call her Mara, which means bitter. Then she adds the exclamation point: "I went away full, and the LORD has brought me back empty" (Ruth 1:21).

And that is how we, I, identify with Naomi. We were all full, in the garden at creation, and we are all empty, due to our sin and the fall. In that little line, she tells the story of us all. Actually, that's only half of the story. Naomi also tells the other half.

As the book of Ruth unfolds, we find that Naomi has a relative, Boaz. He's not just any relative, he's the alpha male who has it all—looks, wealth, compassion. Ruth, Naomi's daughter-in-law, catches Boaz's eye and eventually they marry and along comes a child, Obed. Ruth chapter 4 picks up the story from there. The women of the village come back on the scene, only this time the circumstances are far more joyful.

They look at the child and they look at Naomi and they tell Naomi that this child will be her redeemer, her restorer of life, and nourisher of her in her old age (Ruth 4:14–15). Naomi finds redemption and restoration in Obed.

But that's only the beginning. Obed is the father of Jesse, and Jesse is the father of David. And it will be the *Davidite*, the Messiah, who will be born and who will take all of us from our emptiness and our fallen condition and redeem us and restore us and nourish us.

The shepherds that came to Mary heard it first: "For unto you is born this day in the city of David a Savior, who is Christ the Lord" (Luke 2:11). In the city of Obed's grandson, the same city where Obed was born, came our Redeemer. And because of this child who was born to us, the Christ child who was born to die so that we might live, we are restored and we are nourished.

It takes an ancient Israelite widow to remind us who we are. Her story is our story. And the Bible is full of such stories, such stories God has graciously given to us. Read them and learn from them. For these stories of kings and shepherds, of alpha males and widows, are really the story of us.

READING IN COMMUNITY

One of the things these stories tell us is that we read the Bible *in community*. We have mentioned this already, but in our culture that stresses individualism it definitely bears repeating. By looking to the people of the Bible, we are reminded of the flesh-and-blood dimension of the people of God. In addition, we are reminded that we are connected to people beyond the pages of the Bible.

The Christian community has been around for some time. And it has produced a lot of stories. These stories are for us. They are not inspired stories; they are not authoritative stories. Those labels belong solely to the biblical stories. But the stories of Christian community through the centuries are inspiring and informative. As we "read" them and connect with them, we gain some healthy perspective on how to be disciples in our context.

And we are thrown right back to the pages of Scripture. Read the stories of the people in John and the stories of Peter, Paul, and Mary. We will see that they lived in community. They understood how to serve God as they worked together, broke bread together, partook of the Lord's Supper together—for some of them they had the privilege of partaking of the first and original Lord's Supper together. They suffered together. They enjoyed God together. We are at risk when we go the route of isolated individualism. These stories within a story drive home the beauty and reward of being connected to community.

CONCLUSION

In his *New York Times* bestselling book, *The Reason for God*, Tim Keller recalls the storyline of an old James Cagney movie, *Angels with Dirty Faces*. In it, Cagney plays Rocky Sullivan, a longtime criminal about to face the electric chair for his life of crime. The neighborhood kids have idolized Rocky and turned this criminal into a celebrity. Just before he dies, Rocky is visited by his childhood friend, who's now a priest.

The priest begs him to die in shame, so the kids will be turned away and maybe saved from a life of crime and misdeeds. It's the only way, as Keller puts it, to release these boys from their hero worship. But Rocky refuses to go along.

Keller picks up the story:

> But the next morning [Rocky] walks to the execution chamber. Suddenly he begins to cry out for mercy in cowardly hysterics, and dies in humiliation, making the ultimate sacrifice. Movie viewers are always stunned. I should know because every time I watch it I am shaken and it makes me want to live my life differently.

Then Keller adds, "Such is the life-affecting power of story."[2]

Such is the life-affecting power of the stories of the Bible, the stories within the story. The stories of these real flesh-and-blood people give us hope. We see the power of God's grace transforming their lives, and we have hope that God is at work in us. Consider the gripping stories Jesus himself gave us as he taught in parables.

These stories also give us hope for our children and for our loved ones, for our friends and for those God has placed around us to whom we minister. We may see only hard, recalcitrant hearts. We see no way out. But then we see the power of redemption, the power of God's grace to change lives. We see the power of restoration to rebuild the ruins.

God worked in amazing ways in the lives of people in Scripture. His work of redemption and restoration continues to accomplish amazing things in our lives and in our children's lives and in the lives of those we love and of those to whom we minister. Such is the life-changing, life-transforming power of *The Story*.

GOD'S STORY, GOD'S GLORY: ADVENTURES IN *NOT* MISSING THE POINT

A man can no more diminish God's glory by refusing to worship him than a lunatic can put out the sun by scribbling the word "darkness" on the walls of his cell.
—C. S. Lewis

HOW TO MISS THE POINT

You are about to leave your dimension of time and space. You are about to enter a new dimension, a land of imagination. You are about to enter . . . The Twilight Zone.

If you don't remember hearing that, you owe it to yourself to look up YouTube clips of the 1960s television series *The Twilight*

Zone. Rod Serling will serve as your host as you enter strange new worlds. And as you enter these worlds, just when you think you have it all figured out, you realize, with the sudden force and shock of a thunderbolt, that you had it all wrong.

One such episode told the tale of an alien invasion—this is science fiction after all. The aliens landed; the earthlings panicked. World leaders gathered at the United Nations to hear the ominous directives from the mother ship hovering above, lasers charged and pointed and ready to blast our planet into bits. Twenty-four hours to fulfill our mission in the universe, the alien voice intoned, or instantaneous destruction would follow.

The leaders scrambled, typewriters clacked, couriers ran about. And the clock ticked. When the twenty-four hours expired, exasperated and wearied heads of state held up a telephone-book-thick binder, exclaiming, "Here it is: Treaties for absolute and comprehensive world peace. We did it."

But to every earthling's shock, the lasers charged and sirens began to shriek. Alien laughter punctuated their pronouncement: "You fools, we created you to be instruments of war, not peace." And then the lasers took aim and let go with their destructive rays.

Such is a case of missing the point. Let me bring us back to our dimension of time and space. Let me bring us back to reality. Imagine you spent all weekend studying for an exam in college. You forsook times to hang out with friends. You skipped a meal or two. Then you showed up to take the exam, and you realized, after glancing over the questions, that you had studied the wrong thing. Another adventure in missing the point.

Twilight Zone episodes and even college exams are of little consequence—and I include the latter even though I give such exams for a living. But here's the tragedy. What if we lived our whole lives, even living with a great deal of zeal and focus, for the wrong thing? Missing the point in life, no matter how strenuous the life, is a tragedy of epic proportion.

LIVING DURING TROUBLED TIMES

We bump into such a misadventure in the book of Jeremiah. Paul House, in his introduction to the book of Jeremiah in the *ESV® Study Bible*, puts it plainly and directly, "Jeremiah lived during troubled times."[1] Following the death of the godly King Josiah, Judah, the southern kingdom, made of the two tribes, plunged into idolatry and had broken covenant with God. Israel, comprised of the ten tribes of the north, had already been taken captive by Assyria. Now it appeared Judah would succumb to Babylon.

Jeremiah comes on the scene, along with a few other prophets, to warn Judah of impending judgment, pleading and calling for repentance. The people ignored God's prophet, spurning God's mercy and grace and patience. The people refused to listen; they refused to repent.

One of Jeremiah's calls for repentance comes in chapter 9, another message falling on deaf ears. Near the end of the chapter, the Lord, speaking through Jeremiah, declares:

> Let not the wise man boast in his wisdom, let not the mighty man boast in his might, let not the rich man boast in his riches, but let him who boasts boast in this, that he understands and knows me, that I am the LORD who practices steadfast love, justice, and righteousness in the earth. For in these things I delight, declares the LORD. (Jer. 9:23–24)

The people of Judah missed the point. All of their achievements and accomplishments were off the mark. They lived in the wrong direction.

IT REALLY IS ABOUT GOD

It's worth looking back to the text and identifying the things God indicts Israel for wrongly living toward: wisdom, might, and riches. First, we need to see that these pursuits *can* be worthwhile pursuits. Take wisdom, for example. In numerous places, Scripture commands us to seek after and to get wisdom.

We have a whole book in the Bible devoted to extolling the virtues of wisdom's pursuit. In addition to the Proverbs, we also have the epistle from James. Jesus's own brother commends wisdom.

Might, or as we might say, power, can also be a worthwhile pursuit. If used properly and directed at the right pursuits, might can accomplish great things. So, too, is the case with riches. Anyone involved in any Christian organization will readily tell you how grateful they are to those God has blessed with resources.

But good things can become bad things. They can distract us. They can sidetrack us. They can become the point.

This is exactly where the people of Judah were. They had devoted their lives to things that distracted them from focusing on God. They stopped seeing God at the center. They missed the point.

Even a glance over Romans 1 teaches us how easily we are distracted from the Creator. We dislodge God. We set off in a full-throttled pursuit of everything he has made without giving even a nod to him and without so much as a hint of gratitude to him.

We can drive as fast as we want. We can drive as sincerely and as earnestly as we possibly can. But if we're headed in the wrong direction, no amount of energy, sincerity, or intensity matters. We'll live a misspent life.

The perennial problem of human nature, of us earthlings, is that we miss the point. We take good things, God-given things, and we put them at the center, displacing God and setting ourselves up for tragic ends. And when the curtain falls, we will know we have played the lead role in our own tragedy.

This was the message to the people of Judah through the prophet Jeremiah on the windswept plains of Jerusalem in the sixth century BC. To not miss the point might even be more of a challenge in our day.

WHEN SKYSCRAPERS BLOCK OUR VIEW: OR, LOOK AT ALL THE GREAT THINGS WE HAVE DONE

Visitors to Chicago make the obligatory trip to the Magnificent Mile, an eight-block stretch along North Michigan Avenue. On the one end of the Magnificent Mile, filled with hotels—all fifty of them—office buildings, and high-end stores, stands the John Hancock Center, its one hundred stories towering over all. Well, almost all. A look over your shoulder and you'll see the 110-storied Willis, formerly Sears, Tower. We have made marvelous things.

It is quite easy in our age of innovation and technology, our age of achievement and accomplishment, to begin to think rather highly of ourselves. It is rather easy to lose sight of God. It is rather easy to miss the point. Our skyscrapers block our view of heaven. We draw our eyes up, but not up to the heavens, not up to God. We draw our eyes up to see all the great things we have done. Not only do we have the perennial human condition to contend with, not only do we have our penchant for distraction, not only do we have our accomplishments and achievements that all too easily draw our eyes off God, but we also have our self-obsessed and self-absorbed culture.

Standing right up against Chicago's Hancock Center offers a rather fascinating experience. As you look straight up, it appears as if the building goes on forever. It goes "to infinity and beyond," quoting *Toy Story*'s comically heroic Buzz Lightyear. Impressive. Or, go inside and take the express elevator to the top. Impressive even more.

Then walk across the street to Fourth Street Presbyterian Church. In any place in small-town America, this would be an impressive building. But next to the Hancock Center, it easily gets overlooked. But walk inside and find a seat among the pews and take in the Gothic arches, and you soon realize the difference between being awed by having your eyes (and body) drawn upward by the Hancock Center and being awed by having your eyes drawn upward to heaven. We so need to develop a vision for God, surrounded as we are by monuments to man. Our skyscrapers too easily cause us to miss out on what we should be looking for and what we should be seeing.

We tend to be rather self-focused. Sociologists sometimes call this the belly button syndrome. It's when infants first discover their belly button. They poke at it and pinch it. They're mesmerized by it, staring at it endlessly while an entire world passes them by. It's funny when we're infants; it becomes tragic when we're adults.

If we're still so self-focused that an entire world is passing us by, then something's quite wrong. Belly button syndrome can become a fatal disease. Our culture seems especially susceptible to this disease. We don't seem to have built up much immunity to fight it. Our self-focus causes us to miss God.

HIS STORY

At this point, a legitimate question might very well be: What does all of this discussion about skyscrapers, *Twilight Zone* episodes, and Old Testament prophets have to do with the narrative of Scripture and reading the Bible? I'm glad you asked.

The emphasis on the narrative of creation, fall, redemption, and restoration can easily become another thing to contend with in our struggle to keep our eyes off ourselves and on God. We can make the narrative, the story, about us. I can make the story about me.

In one sense, the story is about us. It is about *our* creation, *our* fall into sin, *our* redemption, and *our* restoration. We are part of the story. God loves us and wants to be gracious to us, and he spared not even his own Son for us.

As evangelicals especially, with our emphasis on the new birth and a personal relationship with Jesus Christ—which are both biblical and crucial—we can get a bit askew in our sense of what God is doing in the world. We can have rather small visions that don't extend beyond our personal spaces. We can succumb to being fascinated with our own belly buttons.

But, only in one sense is the story about us. If the prophet Jeremiah tells us anything, he tells us the story is about God. God's ultimate end in creating and redeeming the world is his own glory. God's story is ultimately about God's glory. By remembering that God's glory is the point of the redemption story, we can keep the right perspective on our lives, and for that matter, on our work, and on our efforts, and on our accomplishments.

We need to join in with the prophets, who long to see the earth "filled with the knowledge of the glory of the LORD as the waters cover the sea" (Hab. 2:14). We need to join in with the psalmist, who says, "Not to us, O LORD, not to us, but to your name give glory" (Ps. 115:1). The psalmist has to say "not to us" twice because the temptation to be self-consumed and self-obsessed is so strong. In the end, the story is about God. In fact, by the time we get to the new heavens and the new earth in Revelation 21–22, we find that the central, defining, and permeating element is the glory of God.

Christopher J. H. Wright in his massive book, *The Mission of God: Unlocking the Bible's Grand Narrative*, informs us that God is on a mission. That mission is to proclaim and manifest and spread his glory to all the nations. The mission of God fuels and drives the narrative; it permeates the story from start to finish.

Christopher Wright also spends many pages showing how understanding the mission of God opens up, even "unlocks," the story of the Bible itself. He writes, "The Bible renders to us the story of God's mission through God's people in their engagement with God's world for the sake of the whole of God's creation."[2] That beats staring into your belly button anytime.

Wright mentioned God four times in that last quote. In our world of the self—we even have a magazine called *Self*—we will never err in overreferencing God. We can't tell ourselves enough that God is the focus.

LOSING YOUR LIFE TO FIND IT

But what do we do with the self? Where do we fit into the picture? How do we go about having a proper view of ourselves in light of the preeminence of God? In other words, we know the story is about God; we know that he should be and must be at the center of all things and at the center of our lives. But we still have to live life, and how do we do that? How do we live in such a way, a living which includes our work and our pursuits, that shows that we, following the words of Jeremiah 9:24, *understand and know God* above all things?

The beginning of the answer comes in Christ's words in Matthew 10:39. Here he issues one of the deepest paradoxes of all time: "Whoever finds his life will lose it, and whoever loses his life for my sake will find it." Luke records this statement two times in his Gospel (Luke 9:24 and 17:33). John records a similar version of this statement in his Gospel (John 12:25). These references leave us with the impression of the importance of this paradox.

We think that by clinging to and hanging on with tooth and nail to our lives and to our agendas we gain our lives. We think by loving ourselves—by putting our self-interest and our agendas at the center—we are doing the best possible thing we can do for ourselves. And we are entirely wrong.

Loving God and prizing his agenda, an agenda summed up entirely in his glory, must be at the center. That much we know, and that much we have been saying throughout this chapter. Here's what Christ's paradox adds—having God and his glory at the center of our lives is the means of self-fulfillment and satisfaction.

We lose our lives, we let go of our selfish and self-centered pursuits and ambitions, and paradoxically we come to find ourselves. Christ's paradox offers us a number of insights to pursue. Let's explore a few such insights.

The first is that God's emphasis on his own glory, an emphasis with ricochets throughout Scripture, is not exclusive of our interests. It's not as if God's glory is a knockout punch to us. It's not as if God's glory beats us down or pushes us around. Bullies do that, and God is no cosmic bully. There is an overwhelming graciousness in the way God displays his glory and in the way God demands that we honor his glory.

Let's go back to Jeremiah 9:23–24 to see God's graciousness at work. The people of Judah should have had as their priority knowing and understanding God. But they allowed themselves to get distracted by their pursuits of wisdom and might and riches. Had they pursued knowing and understanding God, this is what they would have learned. They would have learned that God is unflinching in his faithfulness and loyalty and love. "I am the LORD," the text exclaims, "who *practices steadfast love.*"

Additionally, the people of Judah would have learned of the justice and the righteousness of God. But they also would have learned something more. They would have learned that God *delights* in these things (Jer. 9:24). God takes pleasure in being faithful to us; God delights in loving us. God delights when justice rules and when righteousness reigns.

In no way is an emphasis on God and his glory stifling or inhibiting. An emphasis on God and his glory does not clip our wings. Instead, an emphasis on God and his glory lets us unfurl our wings to the fullest.

INSTEAD OF OR THROUGH?

A second insight we can gather from Christ's paradox regards thinking about prepositions, those small but important words. Let me contrast two prepositions. The first is *instead of* and the second is *through*. Now let me explain what I mean.

We can look at this emphasis on God and his glory in one way, the *instead of* way. Or, we can look at this emphasis on God and his glory another way, the *through* way. In the *instead of* way, we end up seeing God and his glory *instead of* our interests, our pursuits, our work, our relationships, our lives. That's not Christianity. That's monasticism. If we take the approach to emphasizing God and his glory in the *through* way, we see how our interests, our pursuits, our work, our relationships, our lives fit. This approach allows us to see how all that we do becomes not a distraction from God's glory, but the means by which we live for and reflect God's glory.

Christ doesn't say lose your life and you'll never find it again. He doesn't say it's gone. He says we lose our lives and we find them. We stop holding onto them with all of our might and we will gain them.

By enjoying God's world as God's gift, by enjoying the God-given relationships we have, by enjoying the work of our hands, by developing our God-given abilities, we are living for God and his glory. The *instead of* way, the way that sees God's glory in opposition to anything I do, offers no guidance for us in how to live. The *through* way, the way that sees us pursuing God's glory through that which we do, offers all the guidance in the world. Prepositions can be important little words.

THE BROADLY LIVED LIFE

I spoke once at a men's retreat, extolling the virtues of the Puritans and their full-throttled devotion to God. During one of the breaks one of the men shared with me how frustrating it was to hear of such devotion. He had a busy life, providing for his family and developing his gifts and talents—gifts and talents he had thought to be God-given.

He expressed his frustration directly: *How can I devote that kind of time and energy in a pursuit of God like these stalwart Puritans did when I have everything else going on in my life?* I suspect moms could say the same. I suspect busy college students could say the same. I suspect busy managers could say the same. I suspect busy pastors could say the same. I suspect most readers of this book could say the same.

The *through* way could help. The *instead of* way leads to the frustration and discouragement experienced by the guy on the men's retreat. God can be at the center of our lives, he can permeate our lives, and we will find that we still have time and energy for our loved ones and for the pursuit of our talents and gifts and abilities. With God at the center, we live broadly and expansively. With ourselves at the center we live narrowly.

A friend of mine, Danny Lee, once told me why he likes reading these Puritans, especially Edwards. He mentioned that Edwards had such a focus on God that it resulted in Edwards's having such a deep ethic and a broadly and well-lived life. He had God at the center, and it resulted in living for and alongside others. Giving God his due does not result in a shrinking of life. Giving God his due results in a life of wide-open horizons.

GOD'S GLORY AND READING SCRIPTURE

One practical way this discussion impacts our reading of Scripture regards our motives in reading Scripture. If we are reading Scripture to find some key to bring us self-fulfillment, we are likely reading Scripture for the wrong reason. To guard against this, let me offer a series of questions we can ask of the text as we read:

- What does this passage teach about God?
- What attributes are on display?
- What work is God doing?
- How does the biblical author point us to God in this text?
- Even though God may not be explicitly mentioned in this text, how is he at work in what is happening? How is he directing "behind the scenes"?
- How does this passage either reveal or reflect the glory of God?

In addition to these information-gathering questions, we can also ask some application-oriented questions. Here are some sample questions:

- Does this passage offer any models of those who *miss* the point by not seeing God at work and by not focusing on his glory?
- Does this passage offer any models of those who get the point?
- What can I learn from these negative and positive models?
- What does this text teach me about my own pursuits and agendas?
- What selfish ambitions and pursuits do I need to repent of in light of what I just read in God's Word?
- What have I learned from this text that helps me keep God and his glory at the center of my life?

In short, we need to read the story of the Bible with the grand purpose and mission of the Bible in view. That grand mission is God and his glory. In his marvelous and glorious wisdom, God has designed our lives in such a way that by living for his glory we find what's best for us.

As we pointed out in chapter 2 during our discussion of creation and our intended purpose, Augustine was right after all. God made us for himself. When we live for him and his glory, we are truly alive.

CONCLUSION

Good things can be the worst things for us. In other words, we know bad things are wrong. Who's going to argue for being a Christian hit man? The pursuit of wisdom, going back to the words of Jeremiah 9:23–24, is another matter.

Emphasizing God's love for us, emphasizing the personal relationship we have with God, and that he desires to have with us, can be a good thing, too. But it can all too easily become a bad thing. We can so emphasize the story of creation, fall, redemption, and restoration as to think the story is all about us. We see our names on the top of the marquee, in flashing lights, no less. But it's not about us. Who would want to get to the end of their lives and realize that they had missed the point?

The psalmist was right. His words, especially in our day and in our time, need to be heard: "Not to us, O Lord, not to us, but to your name give glory, for the sake of your steadfast love and your faithfulness" (Ps. 115:1).

8

LOVING THE STORY: WHAT THE BIBLE DOES *TO* US

Oh how I love your law!
—Psalm 119:97

ONE OF THE THINGS easily overlooked in the book of Deuteronomy is the command to love God. Nestled among the stacks of laws and commandments and statutes appears the simple command to love God. At various times, perhaps most times, Israel lost sight of this. The law became a burden, a too-heavy load for human shoulders to bear. And yet, right in the middle of all of this law giving—the book of Deuteronomy literally means the *second* giving of the *law*—God reveals to his people the trick, the secret. Keeping the law stems from loving God.

Our personal experience tells us this is true, quite true. Love is a powerful motivator. Why do football fans sit through freezing cold temperatures surrounded by fellow fans who may have had a bit too much to drink? Why do baseball fans sit through inning after inning as the blazing August sun beams down? It's all for the love of the game. Love is a powerful motivator.

WHAT'S LOVE GOT TO DO WITH IT?

Deuteronomy 11:1 tells us the proper order of love and obedience. The passage is clear: "You shall therefore love the LORD your God and keep his charge, his statutes, his rules, and his commandments always." How easy it was for Israel, however, to forget or to ignore the first part. Apart from love, the law became a crushing burden. In fact, ripped from the context of loving God, keeping the law becomes an impossible task. The "religion" of Israel quickly became futile, a setup for sure and certain frustration, resulting in nothing but failure.

David sensed the problem here acutely. He knew the value of God's commandments, and he was well aware of the absolute necessity of keeping them. He also knew the dangers that came to the one who cavalierly walked over the law. He had a firsthand knowledge of the danger. His own life was a struggle, a no-holds-barred fight to keep in line with the law. He tragically lost the fight on more than one occasion.

Through all of David's struggles with keeping the law, he recognized one thing. In fact, he kept coming back to this one thing. If you were to look up *love* in a Bible concordance, you would see a lot of columns. You would also quickly notice that the biblical book with the most entries is the Psalms. Weighing in at a 150 chapters, the Psalms is a long book, far longer than most. It's not an entirely fair comparison. But it remains a significant point nevertheless.

The Psalms have so much to say about love, about loving God and loving his Word, because David and the other authors knew what the words of Deuteronomy declared to be true. If we want to follow God, we start with loving him. We can put it this way: *obeying and following God flows from love for God.* Obedient living flows from grateful hearts.

One of the great texts from the Reformation puts forth this order of obedience flowing from gratitude just about perfectly. The Reformation had come to the ancient German city of Heidelberg in 1518. Martin Luther himself went to theologically defend the city that year in its stance against the Roman Catholic Church. The city quickly became a center of the Reformation, its university producing a whole generation of pastors for the new Reformed churches.

In 1562, the theology faculty wrote a catechism, and it was first printed in 1563. The catechism was named for the city of its origin. The Heidelberg Catechism has been one of the church's treasures ever since.

The first question and answer ranks among one of the most beautiful pieces of theological literature. Simply called "Heidelberg One," it asks, "What is my only comfort in life and in death?" It proceeds to offer an exquisite and profound answer. The answer may well be summed up in one word. Our only comfort in life and death is the gospel.

"Heidelberg One" is famous and beloved, as far as theological texts' being famous goes. "Heidelberg Two" tends not to be as famous, but it should be. Here's the (soon-to-be!) famous "Heidelberg Two":

Question 2. How many things are necessary for thee to know, that thou, enjoying this comfort, mayest live and die happily?
Answer: Three; the first, how great my sins and miseries are; the second, how I may be delivered from all my sins and miseries; the third, how I shall express my gratitude to God for such deliverance.

GETTING THE ORDER RIGHT

It's the order that matters here. First we see our sin. This was written by Reformers, and if the Reformers know anything, they know that we start as sinners. Second, we have Christ's work of redemption, the work that delivers us from our sins. Again, this was written by Reformers, and if the Reformers know that we are sinners, they also know that Christ is our Savior.

Then comes the third thing necessary to live and die happily: *obedient living as an expression of grateful hearts*. Obedience comes from gratitude, gratitude comes from Christ's work of deliverance and redemption, and deliverance and redemption stem from our absolute need as miserable sinners. As the Heidelberg Catechism rolls on through all 129 questions, it unpacks these three necessary things of our sin, our redemption, and our obedience. It's the order that matters. I'm so glad the Heidelberg theologians gave us this catechism. I'm so glad they got the order right.

When we approach following God as a matter of mere duty, we don't get it right. Instead, following the Heidelberg Catechism, we follow God out of gratitude for what he has done for us. When we approach reading and obeying Scripture as a matter of mere duty, we don't get it right, either. Instead, we should read and obey Scripture out of gratitude.

WE WORSHIP WHAT WE LOVE

The early church father Augustine also understood this. We do what we worship, he said. We structure and order and live out our lives according to what we worship and what we value. And, Augustine also taught us, we worship what we love. In fact, Augustine liked to use the word *desire*. We do what we worship, and we worship what we love and desire.

We don't talk about desire as much as we should. It's one of those words that has been taken captive and used illegitimately. When we hear the word, we impulsively think of *bad things* we desire. We think of the bad things we want but shouldn't have. We hear the word and we think of a perfume ad, complete with a seductive woman scantily clad and ready to ensnare.

That's quite unfortunate. Desire itself can be a very good thing. The problem comes in when we desire the wrong things. C. S. Lewis once spoke of this by using the illustration of a child who would prefer playing in the mud over going on a vacation to the coast of France. We are all like the child. We desire baser things when the higher and better things go by unnoticed.

The problem is not with desire. The problem is with what we desire. Don't squelch desire, and don't ignore the word *desire*. Instead, celebrate the word *desire* as you learn to desire the good things.

Augustine and C. S. Lewis were right. We worship what we love or what we desire. We do and live according to what we worship. As we desire and love God, we worship God. And as we worship God, we live the Godward life. We live out our lives directed and oriented toward him.

There are two things here, the object of our love and desire and devotion, and the act of our love and desire and devotion. Both of these require that we have a proper understanding of love. Getting at love, understanding what love means, is not as easy as one might think. There are many cheap substitutes, impartial manifestations, and imposters. Some Greek philosophers spent as much time trying to figure out love as they did trying to understand the fundamental nature of the universe. C. S. Lewis helps out here again. One of the twentieth century's most profound minds, Lewis devoted a whole book to understanding, as he saw it, the four different kinds of love.

Moving off the philosophers and thinkers, we turn to popular culture. Where would pop music be without love songs? What would date nights look like without a good romantic movie? If all we had was pop culture's definition of love, we would likely arrive at an understanding of the concept far removed from the real thing.

Love is a pretty elastic term in the English language. It means everything from a selfless commitment and devotion to a score of zero in a tennis match. And just as the term is elastic, so too our understanding of what love is roams far and wide.

Love is an easy term to get wrong, to abuse, and to miss entirely. Yet, it is at the bedrock of our relationship to God. And I think it has everything to do with reading Scripture. If we're going to read Scripture aright, we don't start with the proper methodology. We don't start with a rigorous discussion and debate over hermeneutics. We don't start by lining up our desk with Bible dictionaries, commentaries, and atlases.

If we're going to read Scripture aright, we start with the words we find in the longest chapter in the longest book in the Bible. Some say David wrote it; some think it was Ezra. We don't know for certain who said it. Whoever it was said it with bull's-eye accuracy. If we're going to read Scripture aright, we start with this from Psalm 119:97: "Oh how I love your law!"

Trying to follow God, to keep his commandments and obey his Word, apart from loving him is absolutely futile. So, too, with reading God's Word. We will bump into frustration and lackluster commitment in our reading of God's Word if we don't start with a commitment to loving God's Word.

ALL YOU NEED IS LOVE

As we said, our understanding of love at times falls short of the real thing. Our practice, our act of loving, at times falls short, too. Part of the problem concerns our teacher. We are shaped, for better or ill, by our culture, especially through the cacophony of voices that surrounds us.

124

A youth pastor friend of mine once relayed the difficulties he faced in helping the teens in his ministry understand love. When he asked them to define or describe love, they could only revert to what they had learned from the songs on the radio. A catalog of answers he received from them included sentimentality, the fulfillment of desire, illicit acts. In short, their understanding of love consisted of lust and personal satisfaction that just happens to need another person present.

You may not be a teenager with your head filled with pop songs about love, but you and I and all of us need to realize the cultural influences when it comes to this basic and fundamental thing of love. Here, perhaps more strongly and urgently, we need our minds and hearts transformed, the old ways of thinking put off and the new way, the redeemed way of thinking, put on.

Let me suggest four practical steps to help bring about this transformation. First, be aware of the influences on your thinking about love. Pay attention to what you read, hear, and watch. We remember the words of culture critic Neil Postman and his crystal clear case for how we are amusing ourselves to death.

Some cultural expressions can have a numbing effect. This is especially true of the pop culture we so often turn to for entertainment. We shut our brains off, but they don't really turn off. They stay on and soak it all in.

In addition to being aware, we also need to be discerning. Discernment is the second practical step. Not all cultural expressions are negative. Thanks to common grace, thanks to the fact that this remains God's world and that it continues to reveal him, we can find true expressions of love in culture. Aristotle's discussion of friendship has much to commend it. A country song about a father's love for his son or daughter can be right on target. As evangelicals we can sometimes assume a "culture warrior" stance, declaring war on all that we read, hear, and watch. Discernment is a bit more nuanced than either blindly taking it all in or resolutely throwing it all out.

Being aware of influences and cultivating discernment only starts us on the path of transformation. We also need to fill our mind with Scripture. Our minds have been filled with ideas ever since we were in the womb. We need to sift through those ideas, to be sure, but we also need to fill our minds with new thoughts, God's thoughts revealed to us in his Word.

The third step in transformation consists in this very activity of filling our minds with Scripture. Paul puts it this way in Colossians 3: "Let the word of Christ dwell in you richly" (v. 16). Read the whole chapter, and you'll see this command comes right in the middle of a discussion of the transformed life. We need to memorize Scripture. Talk about it. Pray it. Spend time with those who live by it. This is how we will fill our minds with Scripture.

The fourth practical step concerns the humble seeking of God's help in prayer. Transformation is ultimately a spiritual work. We can no sooner transform our minds and lives than we can save ourselves. The same Spirit who regenerates our sinful, dead hearts works us over, continuing the good work he began at our salvation. From this transformed stance, we can begin to understand what God-centered, God-honoring, and biblically grounded and circumscribed love looks like. From this transformed stance we can begin to understand what true love is.

Here's a clue of what true love is. True love is more a matter of disposition, who we are, than a matter of mere feeling. It entails the emotional, to be sure, but it is far more than a fleeting emotional flare.

READING SCRIPTURE FOR THE LOVE OF IT

One of the things we have been stressing so far in the chapter concerns motive. We have been stressing the role of love as motive for living the Christian life and, more specifically, as motive for reading Scripture. If we truly love God we will desire—there's Augustine's important word—to learn of him and to hear from him. We will, in short, desire to be in his Word. But that desire is more than feeling. Desire is disposition.

Feelings come and go. Being sad is not the same as being clinically depressed. An outburst of laughter is not the same as being full of joy. Having a warm feeling is not the same as love.

Feelings come and go, but disposition remains. Not only do feelings come and go, but they tend to be artificially manipulated. Happiness, sadness, even "love" can be manipulated. We could put it this way: when the psalmist declares he delights in and loves God's Word, he's not telling himself this so that he can trick himself into it. He's declaring that he delights in God's Word, that he loves God's Word, because *he really does*.

HOW DO WE LEARN TO LOVE?

The question remains as to how motive translates into practice. We could put it another way: How can I have the same attitude, the same love for God and his Word as the psalmist? There's no easy answer to this question, no silver bullet that pulls it off. But there are some steps we can take to move in the right direction. Let me suggest some of these steps.

First, spend time with the psalmist. Read what the psalmist has to say about loving God. And then read it again. Did you ever notice how someone you spend time with rubs off on you? So it can be with the psalmist. Second, pray for a deeper love and deeper desire for God and his Word. Third, remember that love is more than a feeling. Don't confuse love by equating it with your feelings. Fourth, reflect on all that God has done for you. Before the Ten Commandments are given in Exodus 20, God reminds Israel what he has done for them. He declares, "I am the LORD your God, who brought you out of the land of Egypt, out of the house of slavery" (Ex. 20:2). The Old Testament prophets returned again and again to the exodus, reminding Israel of what God had done for them.

The cross is our exodus. At the cross and through the cross, we have been brought out of slavery and made the sons and daughters of God. He is our God, who redeemed us and made us his people. In addition to this great gift of redemption, God has abundantly poured out his grace and mercy upon our lives, providing us all with an abundance of good gifts. God first loved us. As we reflect on all that God has done for us, how can we not love him?

And as we desire and love him, we will be drawn to his Word. We will need it as much as the deer needs and pants after water. And we will see the Word work in us. We will see the Word transform us. Let's go back to the first step, spending time with the psalmist in hopes that he rubs off on us.

ECHOING THE PSALMIST

These verses reveal the heart of the psalmist. Linger over them, praying that these words become your words.

> I will also speak of your testimonies before kings
>   and shall not be put to shame,
> for I find my delight in your commandments,
>   which I love.
> I will lift up my hands toward your commandments, which I love,
>   and I will meditate on your statutes. (Ps. 119:46–48)

> Oh, how I love your law!
>   It is my meditation all the day.

. . . How sweet are your words to my taste,
    sweeter than honey to my mouth! (Ps.119:97, 103)

Therefore I love your commandments
    above gold, above fine gold.
Therefore I consider all your precepts to be right;
    I hate every false way. (Ps.119:127–128)

Consider how I love your precepts!
    Give me life according to your steadfast love.
The sum of your word is truth,
    and every one of your righteous rules endures forever.
        (Ps.119:159–160)

Princes persecute me without cause,
    but my heart stands in awe of your words.
I rejoice at your word
    like one who finds great spoil.
I hate and abhor falsehood,
    but I love your law.
Seven times a day I praise you
    for your righteous rules.
Great peace have they that love your law;
    nothing can make them stumble.
I hope for your salvation, O LORD,
    and I do your commandments.
My soul keeps your testimonies;
    I love them exceedingly.
I keep your precepts and testimonies,
    for all my ways are before you. (Ps. 119:161–168)

In 1 Corinthians 13, Paul confesses that he could do all sorts of amazing things, but without love he's just a "noisy gong or a clanging cymbal" (v. 1). Such emptiness equally applies to our

Bible reading if our reading is not done in love. In all our reading of the Bible we cannot afford not to love God's Word. Simply consider God's love for us. And as we do, we will be drawn to love God and his Word.

We need to read the story. We need to understand the story. And, as we will see in the next chapter, we must live the story. But first we must love the story.

9

LIVING THE STORY: WHAT THE BIBLE DOES *THROUGH* US

Be doers of the word.
—James

The Christian who compartmentalizes his or her life
into two sections of the religious and the nonreligious
has failed to grasp the big idea. The big idea is that all
of life is religious or none of life is religious.
—R. C. Sproul

THE BIBLE IS NOT JUST a story we read. We are actu-
ally called to take part in it. It's not like being called as a volunteer
from the audience for the magic show. It's far more profound
than that. Back in the opening chapter we listened to Dietrich

Bonhoeffer explains how we participate in the story as a member of the Christian community because of our common union with Christ. We learned at various places in subsequent chapters that one of the ways we read the Bible is to read it together, to read it in community. What we will explore in this chapter is how we take part in the plot, how we participate in the story.

We don't passively watch the story of creation, fall, redemption, and restoration play itself out. We're not off in the gallery peering down on the stage. We are part of the story. We're not off the field, in the bleachers watching God bring his plans to fruition. God has made us part of the game. We're suited up and we're on the field.

Way back in the early chapters, we saw how the image of God sets humanity apart from the rest of the creation. We alone, both male and female, are created in the image of God (Gen. 1:26–28). Much can be said here, but let's zero in on a few points.

Whatever the image of God fully means, and there's a mountain of debate on this, we learn from the context that it has something to do with what we *do*. The context of the image of God in Genesis 1:26–28 points us to function. The first time we are told we are in the image of God, in Genesis 1:26, we are immediately told to have dominion. After the second mention of the image in 1:27, we are again commanded to have dominion, as well as to be fruitful and multiply. Again, the image has something, and some contend it has everything, to do with what we do, with our function and our purpose as humans on earth. Theologians call this the *cultural mandate* or the *creation mandate*.

THE IMAGE AND THE CULTURAL MANDATE

To be sure, abuses abound of humanity's dominion over the earth. These abuses have to do with the fall. We are fallen image-bearers, and we carry that with us as we live and act and function. In other words, we humans get it wrong many times. Despite the fall, though, humanity still has the task of carrying out the work of bearing the Creator's image.

I think the context of a garden, which was the original context of the original image-bearers, can help us understand how we are to have dominion. I've learned a few things from my Amish neighbors; topping the list is that they are far better at growing things from the ground than I am. There aren't too many things more embarrassing than having them peer out of their buggies as they pass by our garden. They live next to me, across from me. But I don't even want to think about comparing my garden to theirs.

Fortunately for me, humility and graciousness rank high when it comes to Amish character traits. They only smile politely and wave as the horse-drawn buggy lumbers by. When it comes to subduing the earth and having dominion over it, they know what they're doing. And, while I'm singing their praises, they also know a thing or two about subduing animals.

HOW (NOT) TO CORRAL A COW

From time to time cows make their way out of their pastures. On a few occasions, we've found them in our backyard, one time even having a stray horse pay a visit. Cows and horses weigh a lot. A fully grown dairy cow can tip the scales at 1,200 pounds. Sure, they're docile, when they're in their pasture. When they do manage to get on the other side of that fence, well, that's a different story.

On these occasions, I've tried my hand at being a cowboy and corralling them back home. Bad decision. It's a much better decision to go and get my Amish neighbor and then watch him masterfully, with seemingly barely any effort, get them to go where they need to go. Watching my neighbors grow things and tend animals has explained for me Genesis 1:26–27 and the command to subdue and have dominion.

You don't subdue by beating something, whether it's an animal or the ground. You don't have dominion by wielding a heavy and high hand. You may get some immediate results, but in the end, the ground will rebel and be rather fruitless and worthless. You subdue a piece of ground by cultivating it. This entails nurturing it, providing fertilizer and irrigation. You let it rest; you restore it. And over the years it will serve you well, being fruitful.

Dominion isn't about beating and power trips. True dominion and subduing is about cultivation. One of the ways we honor God, our Creator, is by cultivating his creation. There are various ways we can do this. Artists and musicians can make beautiful things out of paints and canvases, and musical scales and instruments. Writers turn words into powerful, even culture-changing and life-shaping pieces of literature. Leaders solve problems and help others reach beyond themselves for great achievements.

ALL THINGS: EVEN FLIPPING BURGERS

But beyond these extraordinary accomplishments lies a host of seemingly ordinary things that are just as much a part of carrying out the creation mandate. Through college I worked in a bookstore. Great work for me. Before that, I worked for one semester at a local Burger King. Not so great work for me. I mostly closed, tasked with cleaning out the fryer. I think I burned out about three of the fryer's heating elements, forgetting to turn them off when I drained the vats (trust me, you really don't want to eat fast food). It was good that I had a patient boss.

Somehow, though, even that work fit with my task as image-bearer. It was the work that was in front of me at the time. It was work that either could have been or could have not been done for the glory of God.

When we serve God faithfully in whatever task he puts before us, we are carrying out our role as image-bearers. We are subduing and cultivating creation.

The medieval era was the era of building grand cathedrals. They remain as breathtaking monuments to this day, our modern skyscrapers appearing as mere masses of glass and steel by comparison. Cathedrals are overwhelming on two counts. The first is the impressive grandeur; the second is the impressive detail. Skilled artisans working far above the ground floor applied perfect precision to their work.

None of the worshipers below would ever see any bit of it, but they applied no less sweat and skill to the work above than they did to the work on the ground at eye level. We would likely do well to think about that as we labor in our corners. We are not just putting in time; we are cultivating God's creation.

As Christians, we are more than image-bearers of the Creator. We are also image-bearers of the Redeemer. The goal of the Christian life is to be transformed into Christ's image, to become more and more like him. This is a favorite theme of Paul. One place you can see it in particular is 2 Corinthians 3:12–4:6.

As we look at what it means to bear the Redeemer's image, we are immediately thrown back to see what Christ did. How did he bear God's image? One of the things that tops the list is proclamation. Christ consistently, if not constantly, proclaimed the gospel. His proclamation was quite complex, involving both words and deeds. It entailed acts of compassion. It, at times, entailed raising his prophetic voice and challenging people, if not the whole culture, around him.

CHRIST AS IMAGE-BEARER

Christ's proclamation entailed speaking the truth of the human condition. Jesus spoke freely and boldly of sin and judgment. It also entailed speaking words of comfort and mercy, the gracious words of the freely and joyfully given forgiveness in the gospel. Jesus not only looked and spoke with compassion, he also acted with compassion.

Just as there are some forms of cultivation that are more visible than others, so, too, there are forms of proclamation that are more visible. Some preach to hundreds, some thousands. Some merely speak and the whole of evangelicalism listens. Others serve off-stage, in quiet labors. Jesus made a point to say that even offering a cup of cold water in his name, a rather easy thing to do and not a headline-making act, is worthy.

The poet John Milton once said, "They also serve who only stand and wait." It's not just the kings and queens and their counselors who fulfill the task. Even those standing in the shadows contribute. C. S. Lewis once said, "There are no ordinary people." That's true. There's also no ordinary proclamation in either word or acts, as well. Putting this together we can begin to see, at least in broad strokes, what it means to be an image-bearer of the Creator and Redeemer. We can also begin to see how we can participate in the narrative, how we can contribute to the story line of creation, fall, redemption, and restoration.

Cultivation and proclamation, both in word and in deed, provide for us our marching orders in carrying out the purpose God has for us as we live in his creation and serve and engage his creatures. As we cultivate and proclaim, each in our own way, we point those around us to God and to Christ. Through our lives, we make the invisible visible. We are pointers to redemption and to restoration, a restoration which, as we saw back in chapter 5, entails *all things*.

Let's recall the plotline of creation, fall, redemption, and restoration as a refresher.

THE BIG PICTURE (ONCE AGAIN)

The Bible is God's story of what he is doing in his world. It is the story of creation, fall, redemption, and restoration. We learn from this story that God created us to have fellowship with him, to serve him, and to glorify him. We learn that Adam, our predecessor, failed in carrying out his role, plunging himself and us into a new world order of sin and death. We learn that God, even in his giving of the curse for Adam's disobedience, offers the hope of redemption through the seed. That seed, as the story unfolds, turns out to be his Son, Jesus Christ, the God-man.

Through Christ's work on the cross, he undoes what Adam did. Through his perfect obedience he makes a way for us who were cut off from God, alienated from him, to be brought near, to be reconciled. We also learn that Christ's work set in motion not only the redemption of sinful humanity, but also the restoration of all things, that someday the new heavens and the new earth will come to pass and the curse and night will be no longer.

This comprises God's grand story that pulses through the pages of God's Word to us, the Bible. It is also the story that God invites us to participate in. He created us in his image and gave us a mandate to subdue and have dominion over his creation. He has called us to work, to cultivate, his world. He also calls us into fellowship with him by taking us from being "in Adam" and placing us "in Christ."

And we are called to a life of transformation into the image of the Son. We bear Christ's image as we proclaim, both through our words and our actions, the gospel, the story of creation, fall, redemption, and restoration.

This is the greatest story of all time. It is the greatest privilege to read it and to love it. It is also our privilege to live it. Let's put some flesh on this idea of living out God's Word. Sorry for the pun.

PAUL AND PROCLAMATION

Returning to Paul can help us out here a great deal. We need to look at what Paul is up to in 2 Corinthians, chapters 2 through 5. It wouldn't hurt to take a break from reading this book and read over those chapters in Paul. As you read, look for the connections Paul makes between the image, the ministry, and the task of proclaiming the gospel.

We need to stake out some preliminary boundaries before we dive in. First, we would be mistaken to think that Paul's discussion of ministry in these chapters applies only to himself as an apostle or to professional, full-time, vocational ministers. Some of what Paul says here may in fact directly relate to his experience as an apostle. But don't confuse that with restricting what he says here to him or to the full-time ministers.

In other words, what Paul has to say in these chapters about the ministry applies to us. And Paul has a lot to say. First, Paul offers encouragement. We do not lose heart, he says a number of times in 2 Corinthians. Instead, we are encouraged and emboldened. We are so not because of how great we are, but because of how great God is.

In 2 Corinthians 2, Paul stops himself in midthought and asks, "*Who is sufficient for these things?*" Remember this isn't your average Joe asking this question. This is the brilliant, driven, at times inspired, apostle Paul. And he is the one asking, "Who is sufficient for these things?"

The answer is none of us. Not a single one of us is sufficient for the calling and task of ministry. And that's precisely how it should be. We are jars of clay. Limited, finite, feeble, and frail. Our sufficiency could never come from within. It must be alien; it must come from without. And it does. It comes from above. It is God who alone is sufficient. He enables us as he offers us the privilege of serving him as ministers.

One of the first things we see is our dependence upon God in ministry. The second thing we see from these chapters from the hand of Paul concerns the organic nature of ministry. Let's unpack this.

DOING WHAT COMES NATURALLY

Paul presents a view of ministry that is not a luxury, not something we add if we find the time or find the inclination within us. No, he states rather emphatically that ministry comes naturally.

Paul puts it this way in 2 Corinthians 4:13, "We also believe, and so we also speak." There's an automatic nature to this, or an organic nature to this. For Paul, speaking, proclaiming the gospel necessarily follows believing in the gospel. For Paul, speaking comes as naturally to him as breathing.

We can see an even more profound reason for this by understanding how Paul relates ministry to image-bearing. For Paul, our new identity in Christ, brought about by the redeeming work of Christ for us on the cross, means that we are recast in a new image. We no longer bear the image of Adam. We now bear the image of Christ. Paul expresses this in 1 Corinthians 15 and in Romans quite strongly and forcefully. But he also expresses it here.

Paul tells us that in Christ we are "a new creation," adding, "The old has passed away; behold, the new has come" (2 Cor. 5:17). Based on our new identity, Paul tells us of our new mission in life. This transformation is "from God, who through Christ reconciled us to himself" and it results in one singular fact: God has given us "the ministry of reconciliation" (2 Cor. 5:18).

Our new identity results in a new mission for our lives. For Paul, being a minister of reconciliation is as natural, given his identity as a new creature, as breathing. We have believed, so we speak. We have been reconciled, so we have the ministry of reconciliation.

WHAT OUR NEW MISSION IS ALL ABOUT

Paul boils down our new mission to two words in these few chapters of 2 Corinthians. We are to speak and we are to minister. What do these words mean?

We tend to overcomplicate things. We also tend to fill things with our conceptions, conceptions derived from our limited perspective. In other words, when we hear the word ministry or minister, we think of the profession of the clergy. Here's the basic meaning of the New Testament usage: service. Ministry essentially means service.

The Greek word translated as ministry in these chapters is the word *diakonos*. We get the English word "deacon" from this word. The word deacon means service, the roll-up-your-sleeves-and-get-to-work kind of service.

What we've done is relegate ministry to the full-timers. But all of us new creatures are full-time ministers, full-time deacons, full-time roll-up-your-sleeves-and-get-it-done kind of people. At least, that is our calling. Sadly, we're not always as faithful as we should be.

Paul's other word for our new mission is speaking or proclamation. This, too, is something we have sadly signed over to the professionals. We hear "proclamation of the gospel," and we think preaching by preachers. Lots of years of seminary, Greek, Hebrew, and theology. Ordination. The pulpit. Bookshelves lined with commentaries. These are the images we conjure up when we hear the "proclamation of the gospel." Not so with Paul. In the context of his writings, we get nothing to point us to a narrow application of what he commands. We can't get a deferral here by having the clergy stand in for us.

Let's look at what a broad vision of proclamation can give us. First, it reminds us of something we are called in Scripture. We are called living epistles that are "to be known and read by all" in 2 Corinthians 3:2. There's a saying that goes something like this: "You may be the only Bible some people will ever read." That's profoundly and urgently true.

Using the language of the story to get at that phrase, we might say: "Your life may be the only version of the story that some people will ever read." Now that throws your life, both your speech and your actions, into a whole new light. Paul calls us "ambassadors for Christ" in 2 Corinthians 5:20. We know what ambassadors do, making the point of the metaphor both picturesque and obvious. We live as ambassadors.

We who have been transformed by the story are called to live the story as we proclaim the gospel in word and deed. We who have read the story, we who have been brought into the story through our union with Christ and by his work, we who love the story, also live the story. Living the story should come naturally for us.

IMAGE-BEARERS OF CHRIST

Another way to think of this is to compare our old identity with our new one. We used to be *in Adam*. We didn't have to train to be a person. We didn't have to wait to be a person. Being a person came naturally to us because of our identity. We behaved and acted and did based on who we were. We were in Adam and we lived like it.

So it is with being *in Christ*. Our new identity is the basis of our behavior. What we do and how we live flows from who we are. To use the word one more time, there is an organic connection.

In our original role as image-bearers, we had and still have a job to do. We, as image-bearers of the Creator, are to have dominion and subdue the earth. We are to cultivate the garden, carrying out the orders of the creation mandate (Gen. 1:26–27). In our new role as image-bearers of the Redeemer, a role we have due to Christ's work of redemption, we have a new job to do. By looking to Christ, we can begin to fill in the job description.

Christ came to make God known. We read about this in the prologue to John. Jesus came to reveal the Father. He came to proclaim. As we look over the various moments of his life as recorded in the Gospels, we see that sometimes his proclamation was from a platform. He spoke of God and of the kingdom to great crowds, crowds well into the thousands, in John 6 for instance. He also proclaimed God and the gospel to a single person, like the woman at the well in John 4.

He also proclaimed without using words. He proclaimed in deeds. He performed miracles. He blessed children. He showed compassion for the poor. He took time for the so-called marginalized of society. He ate with people.

He proclaimed in words and he proclaimed in deeds. But there is another way he proclaimed. Christ proclaimed God and the gospel merely by his presence as the Incarnate Word. By being here, on earth, he proclaimed God.

Now what are the implications of Christ's proclamation for us and our proclamation? It makes no difference whether we speak to large crowds, or to a handful, or merely to one person. God places people before us. God gives us the opportunities he gives us. We shouldn't compare or assess or ascribe value based on numbers. Instead, we only need to be faithful in our proclamation of God and the gospel.

Keep in mind, too, that our proclamation is not about our profession. Proclaiming is not the sole reserve of the clergy. I know of plenty who proclaim well from the platforms God has given them, and those platforms are not at the front of a church.

And let's not forget that sometimes our proclamation comes without words. We also proclaim God and the gospel through our behavior, through what we do. It's hard to be consistent here; let's just admit that. We all should take comfort in the fact that people come to Christ sometimes *despite* us. But that's far from the ideal. And we should not allow any comfort we derive from it to lead us to let down our guard or be less persistent and committed to our task.

Because it's hard to consistently proclaim the gospel in our lives and deeds does not mean we shouldn't try. Neither should we let our occasional slip-ups and falls set us on the sideline. We need to remember we're on a journey and sometimes we have a steep learning curve. That's why we have grace.

Finally, there is our proclamation merely by being here. At the ending of John 17, Jesus sums up his earthly life and ministry by exclaiming to the Father, "I have made known to them your name" (v. 26). He faithfully proclaimed God and the gospel on his messianic mission. Then Christ adds, "I will continue to make it known" (John 17:26).

After this prayer, Jesus gets arrested, goes to the cross, comes back in the resurrection, and then ascends into heaven. Jesus leaves. That leaves us with a question: How does he continue to make God's name known if he's not here?

The answer comes in us, his church, the body of Christ on earth. This is the challenge for the church. We are to speak and to do and simply to live the proclamation. By the church's mere presence, we are making God known. We call this *incarnational ministry*.

This idea of proclaiming merely by our presence is never a substitute for using words. The saying, often attributed to Saint Francis, "Preach Christ and if necessary use words," may sound good, but actually makes no sense. It runs entirely counter to the model of Christ himself. He used words, a lot.

This idea also runs counter to how we tend to think of proclamation and evangelism. One of the things the twentieth-century church was really good at was personal evangelism. In fact, the twentieth-century church excelled at it. Just think Billy Graham. When we look at Scripture we see examples of personal evangelism, as in the case of Philip with the Ethiopian in Acts 8, and Paul and Silas with the Philippian jailer in Acts 16.

But we also see the way the church is to be a pointer, a witness to Christ through its generosity and hospitality. The church offers a prophetic voice to culture by living according to a different code. The church is to live as if the future kingdom, life in heaven, is now.

Read the ethics of Matthew 5–7. Imagine the witness for Christ if the church community lived those chapters out.

We see a corrective to our radical individualism by realizing that we also proclaim Christ corporately, as the community of Christ. We see the crucial, God-ordained role the church plays in spreading the good news of the gospel around the world. In the words of the prophets, we help spread "the knowledge of the glory of the LORD as the waters cover the sea" (Hab. 2:14). This corporate and communal role of proclaiming does not conflict with personal evangelism. It merely sets personal evangelism in a wider context, a wider context that adds a great deal to our personal efforts.

LIVING AS THE REDEEMED COMMUNITY

We know of what is to come, we have tasted of the goodness of God, we have been forgiven, and we have been pardoned. We know what true love is. These things should identify us. This is how we bear the image of the Redeemer.

Bearing the image of the Redeemer means looking to Christ's example of service, ministry, and proclamation. We are to serve and to proclaim. For too long and for too often we have turned these activities over to the professionals, then simply sat back and watched.

Paul gives no indicators in 2 Corinthians 2–5, the text we have been looking at, that his words apply to a select group. Quite the contrary. Paul would be utterly perplexed to find that we have narrowed down his commands. It's our tragic loss not to see Paul talking to each and every one of us in these chapters.

These chapters encourage us, despite the difficulties, to persevere in ministry, in service to one another and to those in need. He encourages us to proclaim. He reminds us that we have believed and, therefore, as a necessary consequence, we speak. He reminds us that we have been reconciled, and in turn God has given us the ministry of reconciliation (2 Corinthians 5).

The story reminds us that we, who were near to our Creator in the garden, are now far off. Because of the fall we are cut off, alienated strangers in a strange land. Precisely to us, the enemies of God, Christ came with his message of atonement and reconciliation. Christ came to the cross to bring us, who were far off, near to God. Through his work of redemption, he brings us right back into the presence of God. Someday we'll see him face-to-face, and we will be there fully in his presence.

This is the story we read and love. But it is also the story we live. The more we read and the more we allow the story to read us, as we point the mirror of God's Word back on our own lives (James 1) we will naturally live out the story. Living the story will become as natural to us as breathing.

10

DIGGING DEEPER: THIS ALL SOUNDS GOOD, BUT NOW WHAT?

> Your words were found, and I ate them.
> —Jeremiah

WHAT DO I DO WITH THE PIECES?

This four-part story, as we've outlined it, offers the big picture of what's occurring in the pages of Scripture. Creation, fall, redemption, and restoration provide the plotline as the story moves from Genesis 1 to Revelation 22, from the first act of creation to the unveiling of the new heavens and the new earth. In between, of course, "myriads of myriads" of details come at you in sixty-six detailed books.

We've looked at the broad strokes of the story, and we've explored the rich contours of the story. We've even explored what the story should be doing to us. But how does all this translate into our practice of reading the Bible? We may know, love, and, by grace, live the story. But how does that translate into our daily Bible reading?

To switch metaphors from a story, consider putting a puzzle together. Let's make it a really large and intricate puzzle. And let's throw in a complication—there's no box or picture to guide us. We'd likely start with the border, looking for all those pieces with one side flat. With patience we might even finish the border. But then, my hunch is that we'd soon give up on the rest of the pieces. Some of the puzzle pieces might look interesting. We'll study their shapes and be intrigued by them for a while. But in terms of finishing that puzzle, we'll likely never get there, not even close.

Now for some obvious applications. Many tend to read the Bible as if it were reduced to individual pieces of a puzzle, not knowing where those pieces fit in the grand scheme of things. Individual verses from Scripture are intriguing—lots of "color" and unusual shapes. We like to look at these pieces, even for long periods of time. We set them apart, look at them often, and bring them out to show others every once in a while.

Meanwhile, the rest of the puzzle pieces (the rest of the biblical text) sits there in a grand pile without sense or order, and many of them go overlooked. The solution is to get the box and have the picture in front of us as we look at the individual pieces and put the puzzle together.

When we grasp the story line of creation, fall, redemption, and restoration, we have the big picture. We see how all of these verses that we find so intriguing, that we even come to hold quite dear, fit together. The big pile of pieces finally begins to make sense. Of course, even with the box (the picture), puzzles can still be confounding, requiring some effort and lots of patience.

So it is with reading the Bible. We'll come across "pieces" that we can't quite fully make out and can't seem to fit into the puzzle. Don't give up. Keep plodding away and over time you'll begin to see the puzzle come together. The important thing is to keep your eye on the picture, with the grand scheme of creation, fall, redemption, and restoration in view.

The beauty of this story line is not just that it makes sense of Scripture. It also makes sense of your life. Your life, too, may be likened to a puzzle. We look at individual moments or things that happen to us and, like those trickier pieces to the puzzle, we have no idea how they fit into the grand scheme. We question the "Puzzle Maker." Surely this is a mistake, we say. He put the wrong piece in here!

What we need to see in these cases is that God is moving us in the same direction he is moving his world. He is governing his world right down to the details, right down to those tricky pieces, bringing all things to the fulfillment of his plan (Eph. 1:3–14). We, our individual lives, are part of the "all things." God is moving us right to where he wants us. Tricky pieces won't stand in the way (Rom. 8:28–30).

The way we understand God's working in our lives comes by interpreting our lives through the grid of God's Word. Reading the Bible, in other words, is how we come to know what God is doing in, with, to, and through us. Reading his Word is the key.

TAKING UP THE INVITATION

We started this book with an invitation. You were invited: *to take up and read words of eternal life.* I don't think any one of us would argue against this as the greatest invitation of all. It is in these words of eternal life that we find the promise of salvation, the gospel.

These words reveal the beauty and glory of the triune God. These eternal words reveal the beginning and the end of all things and of our very lives.

No one among us would say this is not the greatest invitation of all. Yet, there would be few among us who could honestly lay claim to daily and consistently accepting and embracing the invitation. There are few among us who could say that throughout the seasons of life and even throughout the day-by-day grind we consistently take up and read and love and live the very words of God.

THE CULPRITS

We can point to any number of culprits to blame. First on anyone's list would likely be busyness. High school students, college students, and grad students are busy people. They are working to pay for classes, establishing themselves, building up friendships and relationships, not to mention attending classes from time to time—all conspire to fill up the day. Newlyweds are busy people, but we won't go into detail about why (that's another kind of book). Young parents live their lives in a blur. And the older we get the more responsibilities we take on. I've met many in "retirement" who seem busier than they ever were.

Our culture didn't come up with the phrase "24/7" for nothing. We are busy and our busyness has a way of crowding out priorities. We are too busy to spend the requisite time with our spouses, our children, or our friends. And we are too busy to spend time with God in his Word and in prayer. Busyness stands at the top of the list when it comes to our negligence of accepting and embracing the invitation to read and live God's Word.

But there are other culprits, too. One of these is the "letdown" we sometimes experience when reading Scripture. This letdown can be of an emotional nature. We read the psalmist longing for the Word or delighting in the Word. We read of people in the past like Jonathan Edwards, who "relished" the Word—and we're not talking about what goes on a hot dog. We hear stories of people who experience great highs and thrills.

Then we look at our own experience, and it just doesn't rise to the same level of euphoria. And discouragement sets in, and soon on the heels of discouragement follows neglect. We give up because we don't have the same experience that we read about and hear about and see in others.

There's also a letdown of an intellectual nature. We don't always understand Scripture. We read it, reread it, and read it again, and we still don't get it. This, too, can be discouraging. And again our discouragement leads to neglect. We can also have a letdown of an applicational nature. Try as hard as we might, we can't see how a given text of Scripture applies to our lives.

There's one more kind of letdown. We can call these "spiritual letdowns." These can be played out in a number of different ways. The first kind looks something like this: You read the Bible, daily and consistently, but you don't see the transformation of your life that you would like to see. Take any morning for instance. You set the alarm early, and you even manage to get out of bed. You read and you pray and you feel as if God is going to bless your day. Then things unravel at the breakfast table. You find yourself getting frustrated by your family and you lose your temper. Or a similar scenario could play out while you're at work and on the job.

The bottom line is we may be diligent in reading our Bible and sincere in desiring to live it out, but somewhere between the sincere resolve and the living of life we have a disconnect. We don't see the Bible working as we desire it to do. And then discouragement sets in. Then we neglect it.

There is another type of spiritual letdown. Some Christians tend to see Scripture as somewhat like a good luck charm. We could play this "good luck charm" approach this way:

1. Faced with a problem.
2. Find biblical text that addresses problem.
3. Apply biblical text to problem.
4. Problem solved.

Biblical scholar Edwin Yamauchi referred to this approach as viewing Scripture as a "talisman." We reduce Scripture to the level of magic potion. A given verse or passage in the Bible becomes like pixie dust we sprinkle over problems so that they go away. But that doesn't work, and for so many reasons. And, again, we get discouraged. We face "spiritual letdowns" when we don't see Scripture perform as we desire it to perform.

In addition to busyness and these emotional, intellectual, and spiritual kinds of letdowns, there is another culprit at work in some of us some of the time—maybe more than we care to admit. There are parts of the Bible that make us uneasy. The Old Testament speaks of genocide, of the wiping out of men, women, children, and entire peoples—not to mention animals. Disobedient children were to be stoned to death. And it's not just the Old Testament. In the book of Acts, Ananias and Sapphira lied about the proceeds of a land sale, and they end up getting struck dead—a harsh punishment by any standard.

Some of these elements in the Bible have become stumbling blocks for people, causing them to turn away from the gospel. Read Tim Keller's book *The Reason for God* and you'll see how these objections find a voice today. Or simply spend some time with non-Christians and see what objections pop up. Some of these elements of the Bible are hard for non-Christians; some of these elements can be hard for Christians, too.

We have a whole range of culprits we can turn to for the blame of neglecting to accept and embrace the invitation to take up and read Scripture. We haven't even touched upon our laziness, sinfulness, and lack of faith. Sometimes we neglect the Bible because it is far too convicting. We know our own hearts too well; we know our own secrets.

HOW DO WE RESPOND?

So how do we respond? Let me offer a few practical tips that can help us to take up God's Word—to read it, to love it, and to live it. First, *read*. There is no substitute for reading the Bible, so just pick it up and read it. Let's flesh this out a bit.

Read what is appropriate for you. Some people embark on aggressive plans to read the Bible from cover to cover in one year. They get to about mid-February, maybe March, and then start to slip and slide. Others make it through, furiously reading on some days to make up for lost chapters on days missed. And some make it through so well they do it again next year, and again the year after that. And they will tell you it's the best thing they ever did.

Not everyone, in other words, reads at the same pace, and not everyone has the same schedule. In light of that, you need to find a reading plan that is appropriate for you. There are Bible reading plans from thirty days—you might not want to plan on getting anything else done that month—on down to three years.

CAMPING OUT

In addition to the "read through the entire Bible" plans, there are a number of other plans. Here's one that might work for you. I call this "camping out" in a book. Here's how it works.

Pick a book of the Bible that you would enjoy spending time in and devote a month or any number of weeks to it. Read, reread, and keep reading it. Early on in your reading, try to read through the whole book as much as you are able. This will give you the big picture. Then go back and read smaller portions as you work through the book again and again.

Allow yourself the opportunity to memorize key verses. Think about what you're reading. Pray about what you're reading. Spend time thinking about applying what you are reading. And then live out what you are reading. Share with others what you're learning and how it's transforming your life.

Over the course of the month or several weeks you will get to know the particular biblical book in a deep and meaningful way. This can be especially effective if you coordinate your reading with the sermons from your church, if your pastor preaches through biblical books.

Once you have finished "camping out" in that biblical book, move on to another and camp out there. You have only sixty-six destinations for your journey. You may want to alternate between Old Testament books and New Testament books. You may want to move from larger books to shorter ones. Variety is the spice of life, and variety may go a long way in helping you stay consistent in your commitment to reading and living God's Word.

There are reading plans that focus on the life of Christ or on Paul's epistles. These plans may provide just the right amount of accountability to help you get into Scripture and remain and abide there. The trick is finding a plan that is appropriate for you. We all need to be challenged, but we do live and read at different levels and paces. Find a plan that encourages, not one that discourages and leads to defeat.

Here are some other practical tips that might help. Buy a new Bible. There are seemingly infinite numbers to choose from. You can buy journaling Bibles that have space for you to put your own notes and reflections right alongside the text. Some prefer one-year Bibles, arranged for easy-to-follow reading plans. Others might prefer study Bibles, with notes and other resources handily available alongside the text.

One of Jonathan Edwards's prized possessions was his "Blank Bible." After he spent some years with it, it wasn't so blank. This Bible, a gift from his brother-in-law, consisted of a small Bible that had the binding ripped off. Between the biblical pages larger blank pages were inserted. He then had the whole thing rebound in two volumes. It was very thick and, therefore, not the Bible Edwards carried with him.

Edwards filled those blank pages with his own notes. He was making his own study Bible. He kept it in his study and he treasured it. He would say he relished it. It became the source for the sermons he preached, for the books he wrote, for the life he lived. You may not be able to have such a Bible custom made, but you can find a worthy substitute.

Also, while you should have a Bible version that you stick with, using it mainly for your study, reading, and memorizing, you should also consider reading other versions from time to time. It might even be helpful to read the same passage in two or three different versions. Again, the variety may help you stay consistent. The variety might also help you think about familiar texts in new and fresh ways. So try reading a new Bible or a new version as a jump start to get into the habit of daily Bible reading.

One final tip, *be sure to read the whole Bible.* There are those Bible readers who focus on the book of Proverbs or the book of Psalms. There are those who read the Gospels. There are those who read the Epistles. It was one of the authors of one of the Epistles, Paul, who warned us to be sure to read "the whole counsel of God" (Acts 20:27). We can easily get a little, if not very, imbalanced in our lives and theology if we read only certain books and neglect others. By reading the "whole counsel of God" we can be sure that we are hearing the whole story, and we can be better assured of developing a balanced spirituality and a balanced theology.

SOME BASICS

In addition to these practical tips to get you started, it might also help to outline some basic guidelines for you as you continue your journey through the Bible.

Pay Attention to the Big Picture

We have spent the previous chapters stressing the importance of the big picture of the Bible—the story from creation to fall to redemption to restoration. This is the promise of the gospel, the heart of God's dealings with humanity, and the center of God's purpose for the universe and for your life. Keep looking for and making connections with this plotline of the story as you read texts. Remember not to view and admire this story from a distance. It is your story. God desires that you enter in and participate in it.

Pay Attention to Context

One of the most helpful rules of interpretation that I could pass along to you would be to remember that context is king when it comes to reading and understanding Scripture. We tend to think of chapters and verses when we read the Bible. The better way to think would be of literary units. Sometimes these match up; sometimes they don't. The literary unit is the primary context. That's where we start.

We looked at these literary units in chapter 6, but a refresher may be in order. Paragraphs are the primary literary unit for epistles, not even necessarily chapters. Paul's letters are letters, nothing too profound there. Yet, we tend to pick out verses or even just a verse, focusing on it and taking it *out of context*. Rather, we're better served by reading things *in context*.

The Psalms tend to be units in themselves, which are represented by chapters. The book of Proverbs is made up of speeches in chapters 1–9 and 30–31, then of individual proverbs in chapters 10–29. Much of the Old Testament and the Gospels and Acts are narratives. The technical term used by scholars for this literary unity is *pericope*. Pericopes are the individual stories that make up the larger narrative. The account in Matthew 21 of Jesus's triumphal entry into Jerusalem on what we now call Palm Sunday is a pericope, an individual story, in the larger story told in the book of Matthew.

Most contemporary translations of the Bible present the material in a way that draws attention to these various literary units. They use subheads and spacing to show these smaller units. We, however, still seem programed to think in terms of verses and chapters. Remember as you read the Bible to be sensitive to these literary units, to pay attention to them.

To help, ask yourself these questions:

- Where do these literary units start?
- Where do they stop?
- How do they connect and relate to each other?
- How do they contribute to the overall thrust and aim of the book?

And you can even ask . . .

- How do they connect with the overall story of the Bible?

By asking these questions and paying attention to the answers, you'll begin to make connections as you read. You'll begin to make sense of the pieces of the puzzle.

If context is king, we need to pay attention to the literary context. Verses fit together to make paragraphs and poems and pericopes. They in turn fit together to make books. And books fit together to make the Bible. The literary context goes a long way in helping us understand the Bible.

Context also involves the historical and cultural context of the world of the Bible. The Bible occurred in space and time, a different space and time from that of most of us. We live in a technological age (some say the posttechnological age, but I'm not sure what that means). We live past the Scientific and Industrial Revolutions. The events of the Bible played out in an agrarian age. The backdrop of the story and, keeping with the analogy, many of the props of the story come right from that agrarian world. The biblical world is a world foreign to us, and we should not miss this point or we may miss something in the text. Manners, customs, even places of the biblical world are foreign to us.

Additionally, while our contemporary translations are wonderful gifts to the church from teams of scholars who worked diligently and carefully, even the best of these versions are still translations. The Bible's original languages consist of Hebrew and Greek, with a little Aramaic. When we open our English Bibles, we need to remember we are reading translations.

That should alert us to a few things. First, we need to pay careful attention to the translation we use. We need to do some due diligence finding out about the translators and the translation process of our favorite and relied-upon version of the Bible.

Second, we should be thankful that God has given the church teachers and scholars. These people both work on translations and Bible versions and also produce material for the church. Through their work, we can get close to the original text.

All of this talk of reading the Bible properly and carefully can be rather daunting, leaving us wondering where to turn, maybe even a little overwhelmed. As we stressed in previous chapters, we need to remember that sincere, prayerful reading of the Bible in community (both in terms of our local churches and denominations, and in terms of "so great a cloud of witnesses" of the past) keeps us on track.

There need not be any tension between reading the Bible appropriately or properly and reading it sincerely and devotionally, no tension between paying attention to the rules of interpretation and paying attention to the Bible's impact on our lives. This brings us to our third point—pay attention to your life.

Pay Attention to Your Life

James, the brother of Jesus, could not be clearer or more correct than when he tells us that hearing the Bible, or reading it for that matter, is not the endgame. We must also be doers of the Word (James 1:22–25). As we read we must pay attention to our lives. We may not see cataclysmic and constant change. Instead, our changes may be more glacial and gradual. But if we are spending time with God's Word on a daily basis, we will begin to see it change our lives. We need to ask what impact the passage we are reading has on us. Just as we ask questions of the text to understand it better, we need to allow the biblical text to ask questions of us.

If we're reading the Bible, even on a daily basis, merely to check something off on our to-do lists, then we're not really reading the Bible at all. It is highly likely that God is not all that impressed by our checking off the list. So as we read the Bible, we need to pay attention to the big picture, to the context, and to our lives. We have one last exhortation to consider: pay attention.

Pay Attention

We humans tend not to be the most observant creatures in the world. Animals tend to be sensitive to their environment; even slight changes do not go unnoticed. Not us. While it's likely true that females notice things more than males, it's nevertheless true that we all miss a lot.

If you commute, try to find ten things on your commute you never saw before, even though you have been traveling the same route more times than you care to count. You will likely find ten or more things with little trouble at all. This lack of honed observational skills sets us back when we come to Scripture. We can read and not even pay attention to what we are reading.

The psalmist uses a word from time to time to cure us of this. It's the word *selah*. The word is rather mysterious and there's no clear-cut translation for it. Yet, scholars conclude the word best means something to the effect of "Stop and listen," or "Stop and reflect." Or, we might say, "Stop and pay attention." Don't run through or over words, over phrases, over passages. Rather, stop. If it helps, picture in your mind's eye little stop signs all over the biblical text.

This type of reading is difficult for us. We are very busy people who move at a fast pace. We are flooded by information, by data, by images, and by words. We especially need to hear the word *selah*. Maybe you can make your own bookmark with the word *selah* printed on it. Try something to remind you to stop and pay attention to what you are reading.

RESOURCES TO GO DEEPER

One final word of advice concerns the resources at our disposal. We are living at a time and place in the history of Christianity where there are more resources available than at any other time. I've put together a basic list of some core tools that can be of help to you in reading, loving, and living the Word.

These tools are no substitute for the teaching and preaching ministry of your local church. The pulpit is the God-ordained means to disciple us in our reading and living Scripture. Our local churches provide the venues for us to read Scripture together, to learn what it means for us, and to learn how to apply it in our lives. Our churches also prove the place for us to practice the Word of God, to put into practice all that we read and understand.

These tools below are no substitute for what the local church can and should be doing in our lives. These tools, however, can supplement and support the teaching and preaching ministry of our churches. Let me suggest a core library that comes fairly close to being indispensable to serious Bible reading:

- A study Bible
- A Bible atlas
- A Bible dictionary
- A one-volume commentary
- A theological dictionary

There are many options to choose from for each of these, perhaps so many that it gets confusing and perplexing. Here's a description of how each of these books can help us, along with a solid core I would recommend.

Study Bible

A good study Bible can provide a wealth of education, right alongside of the biblical text itself. Study Bibles offer notes, which can be helpful to us in understanding difficult texts. These notes make connections we sometimes miss. These notes also point out things in the passage we might have otherwise overlooked. Study Bibles include maps and illustrations, bringing the distant past into view. They contain book introductions, summaries, and outlines. All of these study aids help orient us to the book's overall aim and its contribution to the plotline and the grand story of the Bible.

Study Bibles also provide articles on all sorts of areas such as doctrine or biblical ethics or on matters of living the Christian life. Again, a good study Bible provides a wealth of information right between the covers. I recommend *The ESV® Study Bible* (Crossway). With a ton (almost literally) of notes, amazing maps, and illustrations, not to mention a litany of helpful articles throughout the biblical books and clustered at the back, this study Bible has quickly become a standard.

Bible Atlas

A Bible atlas is more than a book of maps, although it provides a large number of quite helpful maps. A good Bible atlas actually brings the two-dimensional biblical text into a three-dimensional focus. Atlases help us see the geographical, historical, and sociocultural world of the Bible. They help us get the setting, one of the three crucial elements to interpreting the narrative of Scripture. I recommend *The Crossway ESV® Bible Atlas* (Crossway). With a large selection of maps and insightful articles and text, this new (and thick) atlas will become a helpful tool to keep within reach when reading the Bible.

Bible Dictionary

Bible dictionaries complement Bible atlases. They further fill in the historical, social, and cultural world of the Bible. We need to remember that the biblical world is a foreign world. When we travel in a foreign world, it helps to have a dictionary. My recommendation for a basic Bible dictionary is *The New Unger's Bible Dictionary* (Moody). This recently updated classic offers a one-volume comprehensive treatment of the peoples, cultures, events, and places of the Bible.

For a more advanced Bible dictionary, I recommend the *Zondervan Encyclopedia of the Bible: 5 Volumes* (Zondervan).

This offers thousands of pages on all you ever wanted to know about the background, cultures, places, and history of the Bible. It's a bit pricy, so maybe you can talk your church library into getting it.

Bible Commentary

The range here goes from one-volume commentaries on the whole Bible to massive, even multivolume treatments, of a single book. I recommend you start with having a one-volume commentary at least. If you adopt the "camping out" in a biblical book method of Bible reading, then you may want to consider adding a commentary or two on the book you're camping out in.

My recommendation for a one-volume commentary is *The Africa Bible Commentary* (Zondervan). I recommend this for a number of reasons, the first being how insightful the authors, all African scholars, are. Second, you, as a non-African reader, will likely gain an interesting perspective on the text by looking at the text through African eyes.

Theological Dictionary

In addition to reading the Bible and getting it (interpreting passages), we need to make connections, the theological connections of what we're reading. A theological dictionary will help you think in terms of tradition and theology. It will help you navigate the corridors of tradition and theology and assist you in putting the pieces of the biblical text together into the big picture.

My recommendation for a theological dictionary is *The New Dictionary of Theology* (IVP). This theological dictionary offers concise but helpful treatments of key terms, movements, and people in church history and the field of theology. These articles can help us as we think theologically about the biblical passages we are reading.

E-Resources

Beyond these in-print resources, a number of resources may be found on the Internet. Here's a list of sites to get you started:

- **www.esv.org**
  Use this site for online concordance searches and comparison of Bible versions. Use this also as an entry into the ESV® Study Bible online.
- **www.biblearc.com**
  This source offers a straightforward method for getting the big idea of Scripture.
- **www.netbible.com**
  This site contains helpful materials for advanced studies.
- **www.ccel.org**
  This resource contains more historical texts than you could possibly read in a lifetime.

No Substitute for Reading

We are a rather blessed people, living in an age of numerous resources for biblical study at our disposal. We should be thankful for the gifted teachers and scholars that God has given us to help us get more out of our Bible reading. Building a core library of resources can greatly benefit us in our task of taking up the invitation, taking up and reading the Word of God.

CHEAT SHEET FOR READING THE BIBLE

The B-I-B-L-E, yes, that's the book for me.

HERE ARE SOME "NUTS AND BOLTS" for reading the Bible. The questions below flow from the previous chapters. These questions will help you apply what we've been learning in the previous chapters to reading the Bible.

Someone once said that a journalist has five friends—the five questions of Where? When? Who? What? and Why? These five friends not only help journalists get the story, they can also help us "get" the passage of Scripture. Let's see how these five friends can help.

THE FIVE FRIENDS OF BIBLICAL INTERPRETATION AND APPLICATION

Where? and When?: Getting the Setting (Interpretation)

- Physical setting
  - Geographical where: Are there any place names or geographical features mentioned?

- ○ Chronological when: When does the event or action of the text occur? Does the time and place of the setting shed any light on understanding what's happening in the text?
- Canonical setting
  - ○ When and where does this text take place in light of the canon of Scripture?
  - ○ In the progress of revelation, as we move from Genesis to Revelation, God reveals his will and his plan progressively. Where does this particular text fit on the canonical map?
  - ○ If we consider what happens canonically after this text, how does that shed light on what happens in this text?
- Grammatical setting
  - ○ Where in the book does this text occur? Where in the literary unit does this text occur?
  - ○ Verses make less sense when taken out of context and make much more sense when understood in light of their contexts. How does the grammatical context, that which both precedes and follows the verse or verses, make sense of the passage?
- Narrative setting
  - ○ Where in the plotline of creation, fall, redemption, and restoration does this fit?
  - ○ What does this passage contribute to the development of the plotline?
  - ○ What does this passage teach us about the plotline or about the particular elements of it—creation, fall, redemption, and restoration?
  - ○ Think of this as a two-way street. How does the grand narrative, the big picture, make sense of this individual piece, this particular text? And also, what does this particular piece, this passage, contribute to understanding the big picture of the grand narrative?

Who?: Getting the Characters

- Who are the characters involved in the story?
  - What roles do they play?
  - Do they exhibit change and transformation or do they stay the same?
  - How do they demonstrate the plotline of creation, fall redemption, restoration?
- How is God sovereignly at work in these lives?
- What does this passage teach us about Christ?

What?: Getting the Point

- What is the big idea of the passage?
- Based on the answers to the above questions of where, when, and who, summarize the big idea of the passage.
- How does the passage develop or support this big idea? Use the elements of the passage to get at this. These include the clauses, the illustrations and metaphors, and the arguments.

Why?: Getting the Point for Life (Application)

Often we jump right to the personal application of a text. Develop the habit of thinking first of God, then others, then of yourself. When we apply this application it looks something like this:

- God
  - What does this passage teach about God, the grand narrative, and his "chief end of glorifying himself"?
  - What does this passage teach about Christ?
  - How does that knowledge impact me? In light of what I learned about God and his work, how do I need to think and act?

- Others
  - What does this passage teach about serving others?
  - What does this passage teach about the gospel (the grand narrative) that can help me more persuasively proclaim it?
  - What can I do in both word and deed that will show others God's plan of redemption?
  - What one character trait does this passage encourage me to work on?
  - What one action does this passage encourage me to take?
  - Based on this passage, is there anything I'm doing that would turn others off to the gospel?
- Self
  - What does this passage reveal about me, my thinking, my values, my beliefs, and my actions? As I look into the mirror of God's Word, what needs to change?
  - Martin Luther once said that the Word of God both assaults us and comforts us. In light of that . . .
    - How does this passage challenge me? What do I need to change in terms of my attitudes or actions?
    - How does this passage encourage me? What promises of God are found in the passage that can give me joy and hope?

In the beginning you may want to keep these questions before you. It would be great if we asked all of them all of the time. Even asking some of them most of the time, however, will help us in reading the Bible. As you discipline yourself to ask these questions, you will find that these questions become habits of reading. You won't need to tell yourself to ask the questions because you'll naturally ask them as you read.

Pay Attention: The Cheat Sheet of the Cheat Sheet

This cheat sheet and these questions of where, when, what, who, and why can all be boiled down to two words: *pay attention*. In other words, if you need your cheat sheet boiled down to a three-by-five-inch card, here it is:

- *Pay attention to the big picture*, the grand narrative of creation, fall, redemption, and restoration.
- *Pay attention to the triune God* and what the passage has to teach us about God, Christ, and the Holy Spirit.
- *Pay attention to your life* and the power of this text to transform you into the glorious image of Christ.

Pay attention. Careful, close, and attentive reading will make a difference in your life. It doesn't have to be a lot. It doesn't have to be painful. It doesn't have to be esoteric.

God promises to bless his Word. God promises that as his Word goes out, it never comes back void. All we need to do is to pay attention to it. As we read God's Word, he works in our lives, accomplishing his will for his glory.

Notes

Chapter One: The Story

1. Dietrich Bonhoeffer, *Life Together* (New York: Harper One, 1954), 53–54.

Chapter Two: It Was Good: Creation

1. Jonathan Edwards, "The Flying Spider," in *A Jonathan Edwards Reader* (New Haven, CT: Yale University Press, 1995), 1–8.

2. Augustine, *Confessions*, Book 1.1. The word translated "restless" is the Latin word *inquietum*, meaning "agitated or disturbed, not at peace."

Chapter Three: Trouble in Paradise: Fall

1. Cornelius Plantinga Jr., *Not the Way It's Supposed to Be: A Breviary of Sin* (Grand Rapids, MI: Eerdmans, 1995), 7–18.

2. Neil Postman, *Amusing Ourselves to Death: Public Discourse in the Age of Show Business* (New York: Penguin, 1986), vii–viii.

3. Harper Lee, *To Kill a Mockingbird*, Modern Classics Edition (New York: Harper Perennial, 2006), 243.

Chapter Four: Unto Us, a Child: Redemption

1. Bonhoeffer, *Life Together*, 21.

2. John Donne, "Meditation XVII: No Man Is an Island," *Devotions upon Emergent Occasions* (1624).

Chapter Five: Hope's Comin' round the Bend: Restoration

1. Langston Hughes, "Harlem" [2], *The Collected Poems of Langston Hughes,* edited by Arnold Rampersad (New York: Vintage Classics, 1994), 426.

2. There is another version of postmillennialism, linked with a view called *theonomy,* which means God's law. This type of postmillennialism comes from theological conservatives and should not be confused with the view I'm dealing with here, the liberal version of postmillennialism.

3. Dietrich Bonhoeffer, *Letters and Papers from Prison,* edited by Eberhard Bethge (New York: Touchstone, 1997), 336–37.

4. From Francis Schaeffer's book title, *How Should We Then Live? The Rise and Decline of Western Thought and Culture,* 50th Anniversary Edition (Wheaton, IL: Crossway, 2005).

Chapter Six: The Story within a Story: Peter, Paul, and Mary

1. Stephen J. Nichols, *Getting the Blues: What Blues Music Teaches Us about Suffering and Salvation* (Grand Rapids, MI: Brazos, 2008), 85–108.

2. Timothy Keller, *The Reason for God: Belief in an Age of Skepticism* (New York: Dutton, 2008), 198–99.

Chapter Seven: God's Story, God's Glory: Adventures in *Not* Missing the Point

1. Paul R. House, in "Introduction to Jeremiah," *ESV® Study Bible* (Wheaton, IL: Crossway, 2008), 1364.

2. Christopher J. H. Wright, *The Mission of God: Unlocking the Bible's Grand Narrative* (Downers Grove, IL: IVP Academic, 2006), 22.

General Index

Abraham, 61
Adam, 30–54
"already/not yet," 27, 77–78
Amos, 80–82
Apostles' Creed, 31
aseity, 40
atonement, 63
Augustine, 37–38

Barth, Karl, 39–40
beauty, 35
biblical narrative, 25–27, 93–94,
    166
Boaz, 102
Bonhoeffer, Dietrich, 20–22, 45, 64–65,
    80
boredom, 36–38

community, 20–22, 65, 144–45
consummation, 28
creation, 26, 30–42, 73, 134
cultural mandate (creation mandate),
    132–35, 141
culture, 52, 110, 124–25

Daniel, 91–92
David, 51–52, 61, 120
desire, 122–23, 127
dispensationalism, 77
dynamic character, 94–95

Edwards, Jonathan, 34–35, 65–66, 151,
    155
eschatology, 27, 76–89
eternal state, 75
evangelism, 143–44
Eve, 30–54
existentialism, 72

fall, 26, 44–54, 133
forgiveness, 62
freedom, 62

glory, 84–85, 111–17
God
    fellowship with, 39–41, 137
    giving thanks to, 37–39
    image of, 35–36, 132–33
    understanding and knowing, 112–13
    will of, 67
    wrath of, 5
    See also kingdom of God
gospel proclamation, 135–36, 141–43
grace, 125

heaven, 73–74, 80
Heidelberg Catechism, 121–22
hope, 61, 71–72, 80, 86
Hughes, Langston, 71
idolatry, 38

incarnational ministry, 143
individualism, 64–65, 144

Jesus
image of, 135, 141–42
incarnation of, 62–63, 100
return of, 78
work of, 59, 122, 137
joy, 58
judgment, 50, 82, 135
justification, 57–58

Keller, Timothy, 103–4, 152
kingdom of God, 27–28, 67, 76–77

law, 119
love, 119–25
Luther, Martin, 49, 168

Mary, 61, 100
ministry calling, 138–41

Naomi, 101–2
new heavens and new earth, 75, 147
Nietzsche, Friedrich, 71–72
nihilism, 71–72

obedience, 120–22
oral traditions, 23

Patton, Charlie, 87–88
Paul, 98–99, 137–38
Peter, 99
Pharisees, 94–95
Plantinga, Cornelius, 44–45
pleasure, 35
Postman, Neil, 37, 46–47
postmillennialism, 76–77
Pratt, Richard, 17–18
prayer, 126
premillenialism, 77
prophecy, 27, 61, 83–86, 107

Puritans, 115

realized eschatology, 27, 76
reconciliation, 56–60
redemption, 26, 60–67, 79, 95–96, 122
regeneration, 126
repentance, 83, 107
restoration, 26–28, 73–89
righteousness, 58, 114
Ruth, 101–2

Sadducees, 94–95
salvation, 63, 73
sanctity of life, 36
Sartre, Jean-Paul, 72
Scripture
context of, 156–59
love of, 124–30
motives in reading, 116–17
objections/barriers to reading, 150–53
reading in community, 102–3, 149, 161
reading plans for, 153–56
resources for biblical interpretation,
160–69
See also biblical narrative
shalom, 44–45
sin, 26, 44–54, 58, 89, 122, 135
social gospel movement, 77
Spurgeon, Charles, 62–63
static characters, 94–95

Trinity, 40–41

wisdom, 108
worship, 74–75, 122
Wright, Christopher J. H., 111–12

Yamauchi, Edwin, 152

Scripture Index

Genesis

1:2	30
1:26–28	132, 134, 141
1:27	39
2	53
2:9	34
2:17	51–52
2:24	40
3	30, 54
3:14–19	45
3:15	60
4:7	46
5	60
11	61
12:1–3	61
16	17
22	17

Exodus

14	95
20	127
20:2	128

Deuteronomy

11:1	120

Ruth

1:21	101
4:14–15	102

2 Samuel

7:8–17	61

Psalms

8	41
8:5	32
115:1	111, 117
119:46–48	128
119:97	119, 124, 129
119:103	129
119:127–28	129
119:159–68	129
139	81

Isaiah

51:8	65–67

Jeremiah

9:23–24	107, 113, 117
9:24	112, 114

Ezekiel

40–48	27
48:35	84

Daniel

9:3–6	83

Amos

7:14	80
9:2–4	81
9:13	27
9:13–15	82

Habakkuk

2:14	111, 144

Matthew

1:1	62
5–7	144
10:39	112
21	157
26:36–46	50

Luke

1	61
2:11	102
2:19	100

2:22–38	61
3:38	62
9:24	112
17:33	112

John

3–4	96–97
4	142
6	141
11:21	98
12:25	112
17:26	143
18:15–18	97
21:3	99

Acts

8	143
16	143
20:27	155

Romans

1	49, 51, 108
1:18	58
1:18–21	50
1:21	38
1:24–28	50
1:28	38
3	96
3:10–18	58
3:20	58
3:21	58
5:1–3	58
5:11	58
5:12–21	62
8:22	73
8:28–30	149

1 Corinthians

12:12–30	65
13:1	129
13:8–12	85
15	139
15:12–49	62
15:22	62

2 Corinthians

2	138
3:2	140
3:12–4:6	135
3:18	85

4:13	139
5	145
5:11–21	59
5:17	20, 139
5:18	139
5:20	140
5:21	58

Galatians

3:16	60
4:4	62

Ephesians

1:3–14	149
2	59
2:3	50
2:11–22	59

Colossians

1	59
1:15–23	59
3:16	126

1 Thessalonians

2:13	19, 22

James

1	145
1:22–25	159

1 Peter

1:22–25	22

2 Peter

3	83
3:11	82

Revelation

4	75
5:11	75
21	75
21–22	111
21:2–4	84
21:11	84
21:24–26	84
22:1–5	74–75
22:1–6	89